ERRATA _____

CHAPTER ONE

P. 5, line 32: "it" should read "they"; "reflects" should read "reflect."

P. 7, line 24: "himself" should read "itself."

P. 8, lines 11 through 20 should read, "This is the happy ending that he permits himself for a page or two as he brings his history of sexuality to a close, the happy ending in which humanity has awakened from the nightmare imposed by what he calls 'that austere monarchy of sex,' the perfect future that becomes the present tense in the civic-minded cheerfulness he indulges in the popular gay press. . . ."

CHAPTER TWO

P. 51, line 16: "motion" should read "notion."

CHAPTER THREE

P. 55, n. 2: remove sentence that starts, "All subsequent citations."

P. 60, n. 11: insert "of" after "citations."

P. 65, line 10: "circulates" should read "circulate."

CHAPTER FIVE

P. 111, line 13: insert "a" after "than."

CHAPTER SIX

P. 121, n. 1: remove sentence that starts, "Due to the large number."

TAME PASSIONS OF WILDE

For Joan:
Who's been more help
than I can say.
love
Jeff

TAME PASSIONS OF WILDE

THE STYLES OF MANAGEABLE DESIRE

JEFF NUNOKAWA

PRINCETON UNIVERSITY PRESS

PRINCETON AND OXFORD

Library of Congress Cataloging-in-Publication Data

Nunokawa, Jeff, 1958–
Tame passions of Wilde : the styles of manageable desire / Jeff Nunokawa.
p.   cm.
Includes bibliographical references and index.
ISBN 0-691-11379-3 (alk. paper)—ISBN 0-691-11380-7 (pbk. : alk. paper)
1. Wilde, Oscar, 1854–1900—criticism and interpretation. I. Title.
PR5824 .N86 2003
828′.809—dc21   2002029274

Bristish Library Cataloging-in-Publication Data is available.

This book has been composed in Galliard and Avant Garde Display

Printed on acid-free paper. ∞

www.pupress.princeton.edu

Printed in the United States of America

10   9   8   7   6   5   4   3   2   1

CONTENTS _____

ACKNOWLEDGMENTS _____

NOW THE hardest part: finding words to thank the people who helped me with the words that follow. Forget it. I can't. A talent greater than mine would be needed to render an accurate account of the help I've gotten from the people around me. The most I can do is to list them. The following friends and colleagues have incited, inspired, read, published, or criticized this book or endured hearing some more or less garbled version of all or part of it: Michael Armstrong; Amanda Anderson; John Guillory; Jack Levinson; Wellington Love; Wendy Lewis; Rachel Harris; Loring McAlpin; Mary Murrell, my acute and hilarious editor; Claudia Johnson; Deborah Nord; James Eli Adams; Larry Danson; Billy Flesch; Richard Halpern; Laura Quinney; Judith Butler; Kevin Dunn; my family; Richard Moran; Lanny Hammer; Jill Campbell; Wednesday Martin; Lynn Enterline; Eve Kosofsky Sedgwick; Margery Sokoloff; Jim Richardson; Amanda Church; Josh Stern; Daniel Wolfe; Richard Elovich; Adam Rolston; Martin McElhiney; Michael Wood; Federico Rimondi; Andrew Ross; Micha Odenheimer; Henry Abelove; Marcia Rosh; Elaine Showalter; Joan Scott; Ann Lewis; Oliver Arnold; Phil Harper; Susan Wolfson; and last but not least, so many students who have taught me over many years.

A previous version of chapter 2 appeared in *Positions: East Asia Cultures Critique*, vol. 2, Number 1, Spring 1994. A previous version of chapter 3 appeared in *Disciplinarity at the Fin de Siècle*, edited by Amanda Anderson and Joseph Valenti (Princeton: Princeton University Press, 2002). A previous version of chapter 4 appeared in *Novel Gazing*, edited by Eve Kosofsky Sedgwick (Durham: Duke University Press, 1997). A previous version of chapter 5 appeared in *What's Left of Theory: Selected Papers From the English Institute* (New York: Routledge, 2000).

TAME PASSIONS OF WILDE

ONE

INTRODUCTION

The most brilliant of all is that story of Wilde's. . . .
Of course it's all paradox, don't you know. . . . it's so
typical the way he works it out. It's the very essence of
Wilde, don't you know. The light touch . . . Tame essence
of Wilde.
—James Joyce, *Ulysses*

SYMPATHY WITH HELLENISM

AT THE HEART of this book is an abandoned aspiration, a "longing"
so "wild" that it is hard even to discern, except to dismiss, a
scheme to alleviate the risk and pain of desire, an aspiration to
lessen the damage it does by altering, without abbreviating, its nature.[1]
The chapters that follow seek to excavate fragments, more or less sub-
merged, of this grand project in the work of Oscar Wilde, a project utopian
and anxious in equal parts, as optimistic as any plan of escape, and as
frightened as any fear of what awaits in the case of its failure. This book
finds Wilde hard at work cultivating and celebrating strains of passion,
attraction, fascination, as absorbing as any, but freed—as if by the wave of
a wand, a sudden cure, or the turn of night to day—from the hazards

---

[1] "Out of the unreal shadows of the night comes back the real life that we had known.
We have to resume it where we left off, and there steals over us a terrible sense of the necessity
for the continuance of energy in the same wearisome round of stereotyped habits, or a wild
longing, it may be, that our eyelids might open some morning upon a world that had been
refashioned anew in the darkness for our pleasure": Oscar Wilde, *The Picture of Dorian Gray*
(1891), edited by Donald Lawler (New York: Norton, 1988) p. 102. All subsequent citations
of this text refer to this edition. On Wilde's proclivity for writing his name in his work, see
Karl Beckson, "The Autobiographical Signature in *The Picture of Dorian Gray*," *Victorian
Newsletter* 69 (Spring 1986): 30–32; William A. Cohen, "Indeterminate Wilde," in *Sex Scandal: The Private Parts of Victorian Fiction*, p. 208.

routinely regarded as part and parcel of such vicissitudes, like the menace to life and limb that give the edge to any thrill; the peril, say, that gives teeth to a feast with panthers.[2] Sometimes earnestly, sometimes not, the manageable desires that Wilde heralds approximate the depth of feeling attached to the more driven kind, with none of its darkness. There are, for starters, attractions powerful enough to threaten the progress of the wedding-march, but thin enough to evaporate before they ever actually do so. On the other hand, there are "life-long romances" that, constitutionally disinclined to end at the altar, end instead before dawn, and therefore long before those entanglements that draw the slave of a more persistent kind of such love to his doom, "staggering like an ox to the shambles."[3] There are incurable hungers of the heart as endurable—more than that, delightful—as they are enduring, yearnings quite unlike the kind of hunger bound to haunt an Irish man, no matter how far removed from the homeland, born in the century of the Famine, the ghost of starvation from which those more glamorous hungers take their form and take their flight. Finally, there is the casual eye for the crowd that displaces and disperses the gaze caught in the act of looking at someone dazzling enough she seems to draw within the compass of her own radiance everything about the crowd that the eye could care to see.

A vision of a desire both safe and sensational is surely worthy to be seated amongst the grand alliances that Wilde contrived with all his heart and mind to arrange. At its most audacious, this is a reconciliation of antinomies, a treaty of opposites no less ambitious, no less paradoxical, surely, than his more famous plans to make synonyms of truth and fiction,

---

[2] "People thought it dreadful of me to have entertained at dinner the evil things of life, and to have found pleasure in their company. But they . . . were delightful and stimulating. It was like feasting with panthers. The danger was half the excitement"; Oscar Wilde, "De Profundis" (1897), in his *Soul of Man and Prison Writings*, edited with an Introduction and Notes by Isobel Murray (New York: Oxford University Press, 1999), p. 132. All subsequent citations of this text refer to this edition. "Douglas was fascinated by young men who for a few pounds and a good dinner would prostitute themselves. He introduced Wilde to this world. . . . Wilde lavished money and cigarette cases and other gifts upon these boys, and cultivated a reputation for generosity and good will of which they took shameless advantage. This was the 'feasting with panthers' of which he spoke later"; Richard Ellmann, *Oscar Wilde* (New York: Random House, 1988), p. 389. All subsequent citations of this text refer to this edition.

[3] "De Profundis," p. 46.

art and society, work and play, ethics and aesthetics: at its most audacious, this is a desire untouched by the long arm of what he called the "tyranny of Want."[4] The very idea: after all, the sense that the things that attract and excite us are beyond our control is as near as we have now to a truth universally acknowledged, so much so that it's hard to imagine that a species of desire under the thumb of its subject as one worthy of the name. Falling in love without the fall: what could it be but a denial of the real thing, an evasion, an inversion, of the awful truth? What is the notion of a desire governed by its subject but a dream of departure from the strain of desire that we all know all too well, the strain of desire that bears all the force of necessity, the strain of desire that rather governs him?

Or comic relief: so immodest is Wilde's proposal to remove the element of compulsion from the chemistry of the erotic that it could only be passed off as a joke. And, of course, Wilde himself phrased it as such in his most popular work, that "trivial comedy for serious people." Consider how far he takes the gag in *The Importance of Being Earnest*, where the most basic law of desire is bent beyond recognition, the fundamental rule that we cannot help whom or how we love; that we may want what we choose, but that we never choose what we want. Here the government of desires by the subject who experiences them goes well beyond the usual tactic of the double-life, beyond the power of discretion that allows him to decide when, where, or even if he will submit to them; here the very character of the desire is concocted by the subject herself. There is the "irresistible fascination" for the name at the head of the play, less like the force of an inherent proclivity than the design of a fashion statement, an "irresistible fascination" that bears all the marks of the choice to be fascinated. There is as well the passionate romance that a young girl confesses to her diary before she even meets the object of her affections, a story of true love that, like Wilde's best one-liners, according to one malicious rumor, is written out well in advance.[5]

But while deciding for oneself what one will find irresistibly fascinating and just how long one will find it so flouts a basic rule of the heart,

[4] "The Soul of Man" (1895), in *The Soul of Man*, p. 3.
[5] Oscar Wilde, *The Importance of Being Earnest*, in *The Major Works*, edited with an Introduction and Notes by Isobel Murray (New York: Oxford University Press, 1989), p. 490. All subsequent citations of this text refer to this edition.

it keeps faith with an impulse to manage the heart as old as any assertion of its recalcitrance, driving to the end point—and who better to do that than one whose thirst for extremes ("Enough is as good as a meal; too much is as good as a feast") he did so much to advertise?—a conviction that men can reform and refine their erotic lives, if not make them up out of thin air. The love of Earnest—pronounced first in words before it is established in fact, a love of the name, a love in the name that transgresses the proprieties of priority, a love in the name that reverses the relation between representation and referent—has proven easy to count as a prophecy of postmodernism, but it is also the final flourishing of what Wilde and others before and since have regarded as a classic virtue: the decadent and desperate phase of the age-old belief that, with wisdom and fortitude, we can bring the universe of our erotic urges under the influence of our own will.

The cult of Bunbury may be another name for one that dare not speak its own, but it describes a different club as well—"now that I know you to be a confirmed Bunburyist I naturally want to talk to you about Bunburying. I want to tell you the rules"[6]—a club, a broad school of thought, really, concerned to teach the methods and value of sexual self-management, a school of thought that Wilde himself, by means of his spokesman in *The Picture of Dorian Gray*, calls, in keeping with a usage popular then, and now as well, by an ancient name:

> "And yet," continued Lord Henry, in his low musical voice, and with that graceful wave of the hand that was always so characteristic of him, and that he had even in his Eton days, "I believe that if one man were to live out his life fully and completely, were to give form to every feeling, expression to every thought, reality to every dream—I believe that the world would gain such a fresh impulse of joy that we would forget all the maladies of mediaevalism, and return to the Hellenic ideal—to something finer, richer, than the Hellenic ideal, it may be. But the bravest man amongst us is afraid of himself. The mutilation of the savage has its tragic survival in the self-denial that mars our lives. We are punished for our refusals. Every impulse that we strive to strangle broods in the mind, and poisons us. The body sins once, and has

---

[6] *Earnest*, p. 486.

done with its sin, for action is a mode of purification. Nothing remains then but the recollection of a pleasure, or the luxury of a regret. The only way to get rid of a temptation is to yield to it. Resist it, and your soul grows sick with longing for the things it has forbidden itself, with desire for what its monstrous laws have made monstrous and unlawful. It has been said that the great events of the world take place in the brain. It is in the brain, and the brain only, that the great sins of the world take place also."[7]

Like a key to a paternity mystery buried in a book of army lists, a novel abandoned in a perambulator, or a baby in briefcase, the rules of Bunbury that Algernon never has a chance to expound upon are discovered here, filed under the heading of "Hellenic ideal" in a didactic tome, far away from the comedy where the mention of them is dropped. Of course Lord Henry's Hellenic oration can hardly evade the suspicion that it addresses first of all, a specific species of desire, and of the species "confirmed" by it, those that monstrous laws have made monstrous and unlawful, but they apply more generally to the category of desire, *tout court.* If his speech admits the implication that those whose desires monstrous laws make monstrous and unlawful have special reasons to acquire the savoir faire necessary to contain them; if his hedonistic calculus pertains most urgently to those, it nevertheless covers all others as well. Like an eye for color or couture, the genealogy of the aim to manage the erotic advertised here is no more than the regional origin of a fashion that comes to cover the globe.

This savoir faire begins by conceding the very point on which *Earnest,* like the most dogged defendant, even in the face of all the ocular proof and common sense in the world, refuses to give an inch. Lord Henry's brief Bon Usage on the proper handling of desire admits, after only the slightest haggling, its irresistible power at the outset. Managing passions is merely a matter of giving them form or expression, just as the speaker's musical voice, the gesture of his hand, the turn of his phrase together comprise the elegant vessel that carries the burden of his argument. Of course, to speak of form or expression as if it only reflects some content distinct from it is hardly the thing on the premises of the premier

[7] *Dorian Gray,* p. 20.

5

spokesman for the other side. It's no surprise then that the work of fashioning desire Lord Henry urges on his pupil nears the midpoint between making and finding it, the midpoint where the difference between giving form to feelings and forming them more thoroughly would be impossible to tell, but this familiar mission disbands long before it comes to the wholesale fabrication of fascination staged by *Earnest*.

Any doubt entertained by the first part of Lord Henry's exhortation—that the desires he pictures have a life quite apart from the imagination of the subject who experiences them, a force all their own that quite eludes his will—is discouraged by the distinction admitted in the language that follows: thoughts and dreams, as opposed to the forms into which they are translated. And it is dispelled utterly as Lord Henry's advice for their regulation shifts from an active strategy of owning one's impulses to a passive submission to them: "Every impulse that we strive to strangle broods in the mind, and poisons us. The body sins once, and has done with its sin, for action is a mode of purification. Nothing remains then but the recollection of a pleasure of a regret. The only way to get rid of a temptation is to yield to it." But if to acknowledge the irresistible force of temptation, as Wilde famously did, is to relinquish one method of controlling desire, it does so only to prosecute the project by other means, this time a tactic rather like the martial art by which one exhausts and confuses an enemy force by first yielding to it. The containment of desire proposed by Lord Henry is a matter of embracing it, an embrace that begins by the act of encircling it within the artful arms of form and ends with the more prosaic act of taking it to bed and thus putting it there.

And while the subject who obeys the call to regulate his desires thus stops short of fabricating them, he ends up fabricating something else instead, namely himself: for a man to "give form to every feeling, expression to every thought, reality to every dream," is to "live out his life fully and completely." To take on the task of managing one's desires is the royal road to the only accomplishment that really matters in Wilde's book, the good work that is its only holy order—"What Jesus meant was this. He said to man, 'You have a wonderful personality. Develop it' "[8]—indeed, its

---

[8] "The Soul of Man," p. 10. "As his supreme artist Wilde ingeniously named Christ. For Christ urged others to live artistically, and lived artistically himself. 'His entire life is the

only order: "The first duty in life is to be as artificial as possible. What the second duty is no one has as yet discovered."[9] This is the design for living that Wilde, through all his costume changes, sustained as his signature style, the design that labors above all to make oneself a thing of beauty, such as the one that the teacher hails when he sees his student for the last time, his being swayed to music, the perfection of his life, the perfection of his art: "Ah Dorian, how happy you are . . . I am so glad that you have never done anything, never carved a statue, or painted a picture, or produced anything outside yourself! Life has been your art. You have set yourself to music. Your days are your sonnets."[10] To learn the ancient arts, which, according to Lord Henry, requires no more exertion than the paradoxical practice of indulging them at every turn, is to eschew "the self-denial that mars our lives," the violent regression to the "mutilation of the savage," the "renunciation" that would "spoil" what is otherwise the "perfect study."

Thus while the "Hellenic ideal," whose renaissance the pattern-aesthete supports with a fervor so unusual for him, may invite a happy view of a perfect world where all passion, and especially the one with which the phrase had become most associated by the end of the nineteenth century, is permitted, it is more accurately identified with a vision richer and more rigorous.[11] The prescription the teacher delivers here for the disposal of desire, as well as the optimism of the will that underwrites this prescription, and then, beyond that, the sense that the exercise of this capacity is the means by which the self can realize himself recalls the project for regulating the passions elaborated by the ancient world and taken up most

---

most wonderful of poems,' Wilde said. He is just like a work of art himself"; Ellmann, *Oscar Wilde*, p. 359.

[9] "Phrases and Philosophies for the Use of the Young," in *Major Works*, p. 572.

[10] *Dorian Gray*, p. 165.

[11] On the specific relation between Hellenism and homosexuality in nineteenth-century England, see Linda Dowling, *Hellenism and Homosexuality in Victorian Oxford* (Ithaca: Cornell University Press, 1994); and Richard Jenkyns, *The Victorians and Ancient Greece* (Oxford: Oxford University Press, 1980). For an important consideration of this association in Wilde, see Lawrence Danson, "The Portrait of Mr W. H.," in *Wilde's Intentions: The Artist in his Criticism*, pp. 102–26. On the general subject of the legacy of ancient Greece in Victorian England, see Frank M. Turner, *The Greek Heritage in Victorian Britain*, (New Haven: Yale University Press, 1981). On other modes of Victorian asceticism, see James Eli Adams, *Dandies and Desert Saints* (Ithaca: Cornell University Press, 1995).

famously in recent years by Michel Foucault, who came to embrace it as the first chapter in the history of sexuality, or perhaps, as we will see, better to say the last.

No telling what the grand theorist of sexuality, the grandest of our time, had in mind exactly in the embrace of the ancient near the end of his: "I think there is no exemplary value in a period that is not our period . . . it is not anything to get back to," Foucault remarks in a late interview, but the austere glamour of sexual self-regulation shines through his wishful vision of a contemporary sexuality, or one to come, in which the erotic domain is gathered more completely within the sway of the will.[12] This is the happy ending that he permits himself for a page or two as he brings the history of sexuality to a close and in which humanity has awakened from the nightmare imposed by what he calls "that austere monarchy of sex."[13] Thus, the civic-minded cheerfulness he indulges in the popular gay press: "Sexuality is something we ourselves create," like "works of art," such as the virtually medieval rituals of courtship it was his pleasure to perceive in West Coast S and M bars, where, under his admiring gaze, the worship of the fetish—a man in a uniform, say, or soccer shorts—is all the more thrilling for the knowledge that, like the invincible appeal of a military title, it is all decided in advance.[14]

Again, though, the agency of the sexual subject according to the Hellenic vision that Foucault entertains defines itself against the field of its opposite, the "irrepressible force of desire and the sexual act," a specter of *ananke* that, by his heroic account, inspired the ancients to articulate tactics for the regulation of the erotic, tactics that lead to a "technique of existence":

[12] "On The Genealogy of Ethics: An Overview of Work in Progress" (1983), in *The Essential Works of Foucault 1954–1984, Volume I: Ethics*, edited by Paul Reuben. (New York: The New Press, 1997). p. 259. All subsequent citations of this text refer to this edition.

[13] Michel Foucault, *The History of Sexuality: An Introduction—Volume I*, translated by Robert Hurley (New York: Vintage Books, 1978), p. 159. All subsequent citations of this text refer to this edition.

[14] "Sex, Power, and the Politics of Identity," interview in *The Advocate* 400 (7 August 1984); republished in Foucault, *Ethics*, p. 163. David Halperin quotes Foucault on the celebration of Sadomasochism as something analogous to the ethics of ancient Greece. Both, according to a sentence Halperin quotes from an interview of Foucault in *Gai pied*, are a "purposeful art of freedom perceived as a power game." Quoted by Halperin in *Saint Foucault: Towards a Gay Hagiography* (New York: Oxford University Press, 1995), p. 111.

This technique did not require that the acts be divested of their primordial naturalness; nor did it attempt to augment their pleasurable effects; it sought to distribute them in the closest conformity with what nature demanded. The material it sought to elaborate was not, as in an erotic art, the unfolding of the act; nor was it the conditions of the act's institutional legitimation, as it would be in Christianity; it was much more the relationship between oneself and that activity "considered in the aggregate," the ability to control, limit, and apportion it in the right manner. This techne created the possibility of forming oneself as a subject in control of his conduct; that is, the possibility of making oneself like the doctor treating sickness, the pilot steering between the rocks, or the statesman governing the city—a skillful and prudent guide of himself, one who had a sense of the right time and the measure. . . . Because it was the most violent of all the pleasures, because it was more costly than most physical activities, and because it participated in the game of life and death, it constituted a privileged domain for the ethical formation of the subject: a subject who ought to be distinguished by his ability to subdue the tumultuous forces that were loosed within him, to stay in control of his store of energy, and to make his life into an oeuvre that would endure beyond his own ephemeral existence. The physical regimen of pleasures and the economy it required were part of a whole art of the self.[15]

When it comes to orchestrating "the most violent of all the pleasures," what might be called the " 'arts of existence' . . . those intentional and voluntary actions by which men not only set themselves rules of conduct, but also seek to transform themselves, to change themselves in their singular being, and to make their life into an oeuvre that carries certain aesthetic values and meets certain stylistic criteria,"[16] are less like what they are in Wilde's rendering, experimental pursuits of pleasure akin to "the exquisite taste shown in the decoration of [a dinner] table, with its subtle symphonic arrangements of exotic flowers, and embroidered cloths,

---

[15] Michel Foucault, *The Use of Pleasure: Volume 2 of The History of Sexuality*, translated by Robert Hurley (New York: Vintage Books, 1990), pp. 138–39. All subsequent citations of this text refer to this edition. For another recent encounter with the spirit and material in ancient philosophy that Foucault takes up in the second two volumes of *The History of Sexuality*, see Martha Nussbaum, *The Therapy of Desire: Theory and Practice in Hellenistic Ethics* (Princeton: Princeton University Press, 1994).

[16] *The Use of Pleasure*, pp. 10–11.

and antique plate of gold and silver,"[17] than the valor and cunning shown in an endless war against the most terrible enemy, all the more so, since this is an enemy within. By no means gentle in Foucault's account, such art is a "domination of oneself by oneself," that can only be achieved by active duty: "The Athenian of the Laws reminds Cleinias of this: if it is true that the man who is blessed with courage will attain 'only half his potential' without 'experience and training' in actual combat, it stands to reason that he will not be able to become moderate (*sophron*) 'if he has not fought triumphantly against the many pleasures and desires. . . . his merit will be greater in proportion as his desires are strong.' "[18]

The dust of all this combat renders distinct a difference between the ancient art that Foucault has in mind and the flag of Hellenism that Lord Henry flourishes "with that graceful wave of the hand that was always so characteristic of him, and that he had even in his Eton days," a difference between "those athletes of self-restraint . . . well known in pagan antiquity . . . who were sufficiently masters of themselves and their cravings to be able to renounce sexual pleasure," or the "virtuous hero . . . a familiar figure in Christianity . . . who is able to turn aside from pleasure, as if from a temptation into which he knows not to fall," and the listless attitude of the semirecumbent dandy well known to anyone who has read a word of Wilde, or taken part in the world that he illuminated: the effete swell barely able to get himself together for his own wedding—forget the Draft Board—the quiescent aesthete whose only plan to seize control of his desires is to give in to every last one of them, whose only idea of a diet is to indulge any appetite that comes his way.

Quite unlike the loose program of Wilde's easy hedonism, the ancient technology that Foucault studies, like the constant battle-readiness that underwrites most classic models of political power, while supple and patient enough for more peaceful methods of regulation, certainly doesn't shy away from the blunter instruments of renunciation, wars against desire, either in a single act or as an ongoing struggle with no end in sight:

[17] *Dorian Gray*, p. 100.
[18] *The Use of Pleasure*, pp. 66, 65.

Sexual austerity can be practiced through a long effort of learning, memorization, and assimilation of a systematic ensemble of precepts, and through a regular checking of conduct aimed at measuring the exactness with which one is applying these rules. It can be practiced in the form of a sudden, all embracing and definitive renunciation of pleasures; it can also be practiced in the form of a relentless combat whose vicissitudes—including momentary setbacks—can have meaning and value in themselves; and it can be practiced through a decipherment as painstaking, continuous, and detailed as possible, of the movements of desire in all its hidden forms, including the most obscure.[19]

At first glance—especially through the prism of the moralism against which Wilde himself waged one of the great losing battles of modern times—the discrepancy between the asceticism that Foucault describes and the updated version of it that Wilde fashioned for himself appears as a difference as simple as the distance between the severe and the sybaritic, between a character strong enough to resist, when the task of self-regulation demands it, any temptation, and the type who, by his own proud asseveration, could resist anything but. The difference, though, between the weakness of will that Wilde wore like a badge of glory, and the strength of the one required and achieved by the austere art that Foucault studies, measures more a decisive shift in the history of desire itself. If the will, as Wilde tells it, is insufficient to stand now against the incursions of desire, this has more to do with the expanded powers of passion that define the modern world he inhabited and helped to characterize than any failure of mettle on the part of the subject that it invades, more to do with forces of desire grown fine enough to insinuate themselves without the consent, or even the consciousness of their subject, like the changes in her blood wrought by virus or vampire.

Her blood? The modernization of the libido, an improvement in technology as decisive in its own sphere as those innovations in manufacture that render the human factor obsolete, a modernization that removes all possibility of contest, even of confrontation, between desire and its subject, is easiest to tell by the figure of a certain and an uncertain female

---

[19] Ibid., p. 20.

11

sexuality that, in the last decades of the nineteenth century, casts its shadow across the path of the strict and strictly male one we have been tracing: the suddenly sexual woman invoked by the techniques of science and the charms of the supernatural, the woman whose sexuality always drives, even as it eludes, her, or, for that matter, the New One who, insisting on driving herself, challenges the agency of a male sexuality whose self-control somehow always seems to require, one way or another, the subjugation of hers.[20]

[20] Bram Stoker, *Dracula* (1897), edited with an Introduction and Notes by Maurice Hindle (New York: Penguin, 1993). All subsequent citations of this text refer to this edition. Sigmund Freud, *Dora: Fragment of an Analysis of a Case of Hysteria* (1905), edited with an Introduction by Phillip Rieff (New York: Simon & Schuster, 1963); and Freud, *Collected Works, passim.* Carol A. Senf, "*Dracula*: Stoker's Response to the New Woman," in *Victorian Studies* 26 (1982). Phyllis Roth, "Suddenly Sexual Women in Bram Stoker's *Dracula*," *Literature and Psychology* 17:3 (1977). Bran Dijistra, *Idols of Perversity: Fantasies of Feminine Evil in Fin-de-Siècle Culture* (New York: Oxford University Press, 1986). Elaine Showalter, *Sexual Anarchy: Gender and Culture at the Fin de Siècle* (New York: Viking, 1990).

The association of femininity and an overwhelming erotic I am remarking here seems an appropriate place to make explicit what I have sought to imply throughout this introduction. The versions of desire that are the focus of my study here cannot be completely collated with this or that sex, sexual preference, or, indeed, as will become clear with chapter 5, with erotic desire at all. This is not to say that these forms of desire do not tend to associate themselves with easily, even ostentatiously, specifiable categories of sexuality. Thus, as I have suggested, there are good reasons why homosexuals would feel especially taxed by the forces of desire that surpass the volitional compass of its subject, and especially attracted to a form of desire that would fall within the confines of that compass. But while such a desire may be especially appealing to the homosexual, it is not his or her exclusive property.

Similarly, while the versions of desire that are the focus of my study are sometimes consonant with the operations of this or that historical regime or aesthetic philosophy, sometimes they are not. I wish to be as explicit as possible here because it will help make clear where I seek to part company from a habit of thinking, a school of thought, really, that has been as influential as any in literary and cultural studies in recent years. What I have in mind often goes by the name of "queer theory," and I will define it only in the broadest terms as a not always coherent convergence of two tendencies. First is a tendency to link sexual practices and proclivities with identity—even when this identity is that which is not one: an identity that transcends the strictures of identity. Then there is the further tendency to link this identity with political and aesthetic positions. Somewhat more specifically, I refer to the tendency to link socially marginal sexual identities with politically progressive positions and an aesthetic avant-garde.

This book seeks to describe a complex of desires that elude identification with forms of identity, political postures, and representation, identifications that have become mind-numbingly familiar, at least to those trained in the fields of literary and cultural studies. As eager as I am to suggest that the complex of desires that I attempt to trace may be detached

Clambering down to the rag-and-bottle-shop vulgarity he is generally fond of disdaining, Wilde's sophisticate falls in with the gauche misogyny that takes pleasure and comfort in the thought that the distaff side is especially (or exclusively) engulfed by the passions that drown the agency of the subject who experiences them. Fond as he is of the case study—"he was pleased by . . . the lad's mad adoration . . . it made him a more interesting study"[21]—the aesthete might be less self-satisfied than usual to see this aspect of his own character show up as one, less pleased to see his own rude attitude toward women cast as an illustration for an entry on the narcissism of small differences, or his derision of them as "slaves looking for their masters" who "love being dominated,"[22] exhibited to illustrate the banal pathology by which a general terror that implicates everyone is passed off as a particular possession that lets him go scot-free.

Those of Wilde's contemporaries inclined to look for a woman at the center of this stormy sexual weather, the hurricane erotic endowed with all the power to blow away any settlement of the conscious will, were typically less composed than his dandy, whose dismissal of her appears as complete as it is cold-blooded. Were it not for the afterthought of her brother, we may be sure that Dorian Gray would have kept his promise to the girl he coaxed to suicide, and never given her another thought himself, not like that physician of the psyche whom all the scientific distance in the world couldn't save from the specter of the female sexuality that got away. And Freud himself is cool by comparison to others, where something like the fever that marks conversion attends the anxiety of infection or affliction by female sexuality that courses through the more lurid literature of the fin de siècle—*Dracula*: " 'Arthur! Oh my love, I am so glad you have come! Kiss me!' "; "my eyes opened involuntarily. . . . I felt in my heart a wicked burning desire that they would kiss me with those red lips."[23]

The anxiety exhibited here, the male anxiety in which the fear of feminization merges with the fear of pacification, is hardly new to the

---

from those particularities with which they have been most often spotted by recent criticism, I am no less eager to make clear the connection between this complex and another particularity: namely, the historical epoch that social theorists call modernity.

[21] *Dorian Gray*, p. 48.
[22] Ibid., p. 81.
[23] *Dracula*, pp. 53, 208.

13

late nineteenth century. Thus Roland Barthes can observe on the broad category of modern love: "there is an odd turnabout here: in the ancient myth, the ravisher is active, he wants to seize his prey, he is the subject of the rape (of which the object is a Woman, as we know, invariably passive); in the modern myth (that of love-as-passion), the contrary is the case. . . . the lover [is] the one who has been ravished . . . captured and enchanted . . . always implicitly feminized."[24]

No doubt, though, that the fear of female sexuality was especially gaudy in the late nineteenth century and that this fear signifies a constitutional crisis for the male subject, whose sexual self-management has been our concern so far. While the armies of desire the ancients confront in Foucault's history—awesome always, sometimes overpowering—always leave the subject they assault with resources to respond, the brand of desire Wilde was obliged to admit into the work, into the life (we may know it better by its more authoritative cognates: libidinal instinct, sexual drive), annuls altogether the margin of volition by which he can determine at least how to dispose of it. Listen to the Hellenic orator change his tune by the time he is done in *Dorian Gray*, relinquishing even the light hold over desire afforded by his curriculum when he first introduced it. Scorning Dorian Gray's resolution at the end of the novel to forgo despoiling a nearby milkmaid, he begins with the same theme as before—the futility and uglifying effects of renunciation—but this time leaves off the happy hygienic ending, in which the inevitable giving-in to impulses turns out to be the means of getting over them. This time, there is only the helplessness of the self, ambushed by passions that were supposed to be spent, but, as it turns out, were only playing possum after all:

> Dorian, don't deceive yourself. Life is not governed by will or intention. Life is a question of nerves and fibres, and slowly built-up cells in which thought hides itself and passion has its dreams. You may fancy yourself safe, and think yourself strong. But a chance tone of colour in a room or a morning sky, a particular perfume that you had once loved and that brings subtle memories with it, a line from a forgotten poem that you had come across again, a cadence from a piece of music that you had ceased to play—I tell you, Dorian,

[24] Roland Barthes, *A Lover's Discourse: Fragments*, translated by Richard Howard (New York: Farrar, Straus and Giroux, 1978), p. 188–89.

that it is on things like these that our lives depend. Browning writes about that somewhere, but our own senses will imagine them for us. There are moments when the odour of lilas blanc passes suddenly across me, and I have to live the strangest month of my life over again.[25]

With the light touch of a casual addendum, Lord Henry pulls down the single pillar of his Hellenic ideal: the sole measure of discretionary control held by its subject of desire—the power to punctuate it—slips through his fingers here: he is as helpless now to end it as he was to refuse it in the first place. Thus the entire kingdom of temptation now joins the lingering spirit of the renounced impulse; no less than those that we sought to resist, the memories of those we didn't keep their hold over us, or rather, the invisible traces of them—the memory of experiences carried and characterized by a perfume you once loved, a line from a poem you forgot, a cadence from a piece of music you had ceased to play. More than that, desire—thoughts and passions kin to those for the milkmaid, only too deep or disgraceful for words—is concealed now in "nerves and fibers, and slowly built-up cells," a crypt from which the subject who bears it is quite shut out. And now the life realized as a work of art by the subject who submits to the exercise of embracing his desires passes away, leaving in his place a diminished thing, as exposed as an open vessel to the influences exerted by the work of art, but no longer one himself. At least, and we will return to this qualification a little later, it is no longer one that he has made himself, since the disposition of his desire is now decided elsewhere entirely, decided by the thought and passions associated or identified with it; the thought that "hides itself," the passion that "has its dreams."

Of course, there is nothing exceptional about the measure Wilde takes of a world where one's desires are beyond his control: his assessment is quite in line not only with the alarm of contemporary sensibilities, but also the abstract conceptions of contemporary science, and of course one in particular. It seems to me that no one who has ever heard of it can help but hear in the great aesthete's final confession the basic language of psychoanalysis, which assigns the disposition of our desire to agencies as removed from our own conscious intention as the most distant planet, all

[25] *Dorian Gray*, p. 165.

the while dwelling nearer than what is closest to home, agencies that, along with the "ideational presentations" of the "instinctual impulses" that they regulate, perform their operations under the cover of the unconscious.[26] What Lord Henry calls the "thought [that] hides itself" is divided in Freud between the hidden thought and the hidden things that hide it, a government no less foreign for the fact that it dwells within, an occupying force that renders the ethos of self-control as obsolete as devotion to a pagan deity: or, to recall the analogy that Freud himself preferred, a vision of our own little world as the center of the entire solar system.[27]

If there is nothing exceptional about the measure Wilde takes of a world where one's desires are beyond his control, if such a conception of desire is the most common sense of the world we know, what about his obvious pleasure in announcing it? The moralistic misprision that would take Wilde to task for malingering, even though strenuous exertion has ceased to be relevant, might be on stronger ground with the sense that his concession of defeat by the forces of desire is really a celebration of it, a gleeful embrace rather than a grim admission. Again, though, Wilde is hardly the only one: for whom is the surrender he celebrates not, at least

---

[26] Sigmund Freud, "The Unconscious," in *General Psychological Theory: Papers on Metapsychology*, edited with an Introduction by Phillip Rieff (New York: Macmillan, 1963), p. 126.

[27] "In the course of centuries the naive self-love of men has had to submit to two major blows at the hands of science. The first was when they learnt that our earth was not the center of the universe but only a tiny fragment of a cosmic system of scarcely imaginable vastness. This is associated in our minds with the name of Copernicus. . . . The second blow fell when biological research destroyed man's supposedly privileged place in creation and proved his descent from the animal kingdom and his ineradicable animal nature. This revaluation has been accomplished in our own days by Darwin, Wallace and their predecessors, though not without the most violent contemporary opposition. But human megalomania will have suffered its third and most wounding blow from the psychological research of the present time which seeks to prove to the ego that it is not even master of its own house, but must content itself with scanty information of what is going on unconsciously in its mind"; Lecture XVIII in Sigmund Freud, *Introductory Lectures on Psychoanalysis* (1917), edited and translated by James Strachey (New York: Norton, 1966), p. 284–85. In the years since Freud wrote, the gap between the will of the self and the determination of what he wants has only seemed to widen as the shadow of the conscious ego that can be discerned in Freud's account of the unconscious agency charged with the conduct of desire dissolves into structures even more aloof from the subject—the inhuman mechanisms of the linguistic, according to a well-known train of thought within psychoanalysis itself. See Jacques Lacan, *The Four Fundamental Concepts of Psycho-Analysis*, edited by Jacques-Alain Miller, translated by Alan Sheridan (New York: Norton, 1978); *Ecrits*, translated by Alan Sheridan (New York: Norton, 1977).

sometimes, a thing of joy, surrender like the submission to an involuntary memory, as irresistible as the rapture it recalls, induced by the fragrant odor or the fine line?

REACTION FORMATION AS SOCIAL FORM

Except when he feels like it, of course, Wilde is the last person in the world to take all this lying down. The chapters that follow study the methods and materials by which Wilde seeks to counteract forces of temptation formidable enough to make the very idea of resistance to them a farce, the ideal of managing them a self-flattering illusion. There is first of all the categorical denial of these forces in *Earnest*, the dramatic reversal we have already reviewed that subordinates the power of attraction to the character who suffers it, the practically Ptolemaic rationalization—leaving aside rationalizations closer to hand—by which desire is actually decided by the subject who would appear by the lights of the naked eye to be compelled by it. (As we will see in the next chapter, this conception of malleable desire shows up in the oddest places on the cultural map that Wilde helped to illuminate: the subject keen enough to design her own desire takes her cue from a vision of the Orient that Wilde, among others, regards as a work of art.)

But like the grief we remember when we laugh, the familiar figure of a desire out of our control bleeds through the inverted image of the spectacular character who, in his triumphant comedy, has all his proclivities well in hand.[28] Like everyone else who lives in the world we know, Wilde is in no position to restrict his relations with the tyranny of want to the simple super-power foreign policy of nonrecognition. The art of desire that would script the shape of our passions, or even the art of the self that would cast our management of more obdurate yearnings as the

---

[28] "A steady course of Balzac reduces our living friends to shadows, and our acquaintances to the shadows of shades. His characters have a kind of fervent fiery-coloured existence. They dominate us, and defy scepticism. One of the great tragedies of my life is the death of Lucien de Rubempre. It is a grief from which I have never been able to completely rid myself. It haunts me in my moments of pleasure. I remember it when I laugh." Wilde, "The Decay of Lying," in *The Artist as Critic: Critical Writings of Oscar Wilde*, edited by Richard Ellmann (Chicago: University of Chicago Press, 1969), p. 299.

currency of a personal style, are as trivial as the merest whim in a world where our attractions have assumed the magnetism and magnitude of a hidden god or a law of nature.

No less legible as a means of escape from a universe where people are helpless to resist or regulate their attractions than a fictional world where this law of desire is annulled is a certain stylization of the self that Wilde famously celebrated. Giving Caesar his due, ceding the ground that the ancient ideal held out as the field of play where one fashions oneself to the rule of forces beyond our control, Wilde pictures another labor of self-fashioning instead, the labor of self fashioning which appears at its most glamorous in the labor of fashion itself. Those who have most famously studied this art of the self categorize it as the fruit of the freedom that attends modernity—the loosening of the traditional bonds that once constituted our identity, the style of life that bears the mark of a personal signature rather than an imposed status.[29] It is Wilde, of all people, who discerns the shades of an iron cage in the midst of all this freedom, an iron cage that somehow eluded graver thinkers: if the flowering of such style is grounded in a freedom attached to the modern world, its flourishing is aided by the pressure of a tyranny attached to modern times as well. The art of personal expression that Wilde advocates provides, amongst other things, a distraction from the tyranny that assigns the power to determine the expression of desire to agencies quite alien to the self—the offices of repression, in all its fine and intricate aspects, the complex transformational grammars Freud called by various names: distortion, condensation, reversal, displacement, sublimation, negation, to mention a few. The niceties of this masquerade might draw a look of admiration from even the most studied character in the society play, were it not that such brilliant society is accustomed to give credit for these accomplish-

[29] Georg Simmel, "The Style of Life," in *The Philosophy of Money* (1900), edited by David Frisby, translated by Tom Bottomore and David Frisby (New York: Routledge: 1991). Friedrich Nietzsche, *Basic Writings of Nietzsche* (New York: Modern Library, 1968). Georg Simmel, *Schopenhauer and Nietzsche* (1907), translated by Helmut Loiskandl (Amherst: University of Massachusetts Press, 1986). Alexander Nehamas, *Nietzsche: Life as Literature* (Cambridge: Harvard University Press, 1985). On the general relation of modernity and personal autonomy, see Emile Durkheim, *The Division of Labor in Society* (1893) (New York: Free Press, 1984).

ments to the conscious contrivance of a player consciously inspired, at least apparently so, by it—all the style of flirtation, say[30]—rather than an array of intricate operations concealed from him: "In this matter a delicate balancing takes place, the play of which is hidden from us."[31]

Consider the damage done to the "art of the self" we have been studying, whose student, by the practice of suspending, seizing, shaping, and sublimating his erotic passions, sets his life to music and makes his days into sonnets. Taken out of his hands now by new management, this drama of self-realization by which, in the words of Wilde's very own Lord Henry, he is "elevated and made keen" is thus abruptly closed down.[32] There is the arrest of his development, and then, of course, there is his possible arrest. The beautiful life of a Dorian Gray is menaced by hazards more pressing than those that would blunt, like the sudden case of nerves that spoils the dance step, the fine style of self-regulation. Listen one last time to the Hellenic oration, this time with the caveats restored:

> The aim of life is self-development. To realize one's nature perfectly—that is what each of us is here for. People are afraid of themselves, nowadays. They have forgotten the highest of duties, the duty that one owes to one's self. . . . Courage has gone out of the race. Perhaps we never really had it. The terror of society, which is the basis of morals, the terror of God, which is the secret of religion. These are the . . . things that govern us. . . . And yet I believe that if one man were to live out his life fully and completely, were to give form to every feeling, expression to every thought, reality to every dream—I believe that the world would gain such a fresh impulse of joy that we would forget all the maladies of mediaevalism, and return to the Hellenic ideal.[33]

---

[30] On flirtation as a performance determined by the conscious labor of the subject who performs it, see Simmel on "Sociability," in *The Sociology of Georg Simmel*, translated, edited, and with an Introduction by Kurt H. Wolff (New York: Free Press, 1950), pp. 40–57. All subsequent citations of this text are from this edition.

[31] Freud, "Repression," in *General Psychological Theory*, p. 108.

[32] "There come [occasions] . . . from time to time . . . in which the thoughts of men draw nearer together than is their wont. . . . Here, artists and philosophers and those whom the action of the world has elevated and made keen, do not live in isolation, but breathe a common air, and catch light and heat from each other's thoughts"; Walter Pater, *The Renaissance* (1873), edited with an Introduction and Notes by Adam Phillips (Oxford: Oxford University Press, 1998), p. xxxiii.

[33] Wilde, *Dorian Gray*, p. 20.

Who better to appreciate the perilous state of a life that has lost control over the form and expression of desire than Wilde: "To be despised, mocked, abandoned, sneered at—to be an outcast! To find the door shut against one, to have to creep in by hideous byways, afraid every moment lest the mask should be stripped from one's face, and all the while to hear the laughter, the horrible laughter of the world, a thing more tragic than all the tears the world has ever shed."[34] At the heart of this terror, of course, is the love that dare not speak its name—or perhaps, by now, the love that need not. If we are ever disinclined to mention it now when Wilde's name comes up, or more broadly, for that matter, whenever the topic arises of any desire sufficiently troubling to society that those implicated expose themselves to all sorts of trouble for it—"The world mocks at it and sometimes puts one in the pillory for it"[35]—this may be less because we dare not speak it than that we may be weary of speaking about so little else.

In any case, though, it's hard not to hear a note on the author through the speech of his melodramatic heroine however powerful the urge of this author to detach himself from the subjection of women— manifestly hard for Wilde himself, who, in the letter from prison, takes the sentences he ascribes to her to describe his own.[36] It's hard not to hear the charge of the love that dare not speak its name in all the circuits of passion that run through the novel that helped to make those charges stick: the "day-dreams and sleeping dreams" of a boy, whose mere memory might stain" his "cheek with shame."[37]

It may be worth noting that the subject whose helplessness to determine the form and expression of his desires has a kind of revenge in the diminished epistemological capacity of those who would read her:

CECILY: You must not laugh at me, darling, but it had always been a girlish
  dream of mine to love someone whose name was Ernest . . .

[34] Wilde, *Lady Windermere's Fan*, in *Major Works*, p. 367.
[35] This is a sentence from Wilde's famous speech on the "love that dare not speak its name" at the first trial. Quoted in Ellmann, *Oscar Wilde*, p. 463.
[36] "De Profundis," pp. 129–30.
[37] *Dorian Gray*, p. 20.

ALGERNON: But my dear child, do you mean to say you could not love me if I had some other name?

CECILY: I might respect you . . . I might admire your character, but I fear that I should not be able to give you my undivided attention.[38]

Were it not for the fact that it's the merest whim to begin with, dropped on the way to the altar as easily as it was picked up in the first place, Cecily's stated preference would keep her from reaching it, for a simple reason easily missed in the mass movement toward it in the end: that her own partner doesn't actually possess that certain something necessary to generate a love good enough to get her there. Were it not for that, her lot would be a life of "passionate celibacy"[39] like the one for which a Don and a Cardinal felt pressed to apologize,[40] as distant from the nuptial bar as the train-station indiscretion that Lady Bracknell attributes to Ernest, as distant from the matrimonial union as the ones that take place on the train platform where she almost inexplicably fears that she will be subjected to comment: "Come, dear . . . we have already missed five, if not six, trains. To miss any more might expose us to comment on the platform."[41]—as distant from the canonically approved alliance as Algernon arranges to be when, by the alibi of his false friend Bunbury, he pursues intrigues quite removed from the dull spectacle of married couples washing their clean linen in public, as distant as the pursuits of pleasure whose souvenirs include tellingly inscribed cigarette cases that find their way into the hands of blackmailers out for fun or money.

Thus the symptoms of the homosexual are all over the whole category of desire that opposes what, in certain circles, now goes by the name of "heterosexual normativity," symptoms masked by a cultural censorship—the regulative agency of repression writ large—that requires that any expression of such desire that passes into general circulation, even amidst those who call their own "family values"—does so as always deniable subtext. Why, even Basil Hallward's confession wouldn't stand up in

[38] *Earnest*, p. 514.

[39] Ibid. p. 532.

[40] On the implications of homosexuality attached to the "passionate celibacy" of Pater and Newman, see Richard Ellmann and Ellis Hanson, *Decadence and Catholicism*, (Cambridge: Harvard University Press, 1997).

[41] *Earnest*, p. 533.

court, followed as it is by the most familiar formula for the denial of sexuality: "He is never more present in my work than when no image of him is there. He is a suggestion, as I have said, of a new manner. I find him in the curves of certain lines, in the loveliness and subtleties of certain colours. That is all."[42]

In recent years all the liveliest essays given over to the study of the homosexuality expressed under the pressure of homophobic persecution locate it in the underground semiotic network that one critic felicitously deems "the shadow kingdom of connotation."[43] Not content to insinuate itself here and there in this and that double entendre, this or that uncertain reference, homosexual desire, by the measure of what has come to call itself "queer theory," takes over the categories of insinuation and uncertainty, entirely. Thus, Christopher Craft: "That Wilde achieves these critical effects without the slightest breach in heterosexual decorum—that *Earnest* remains for 'our' critical tradition a readily consumable straight play—is not the least measure of a genius whose wile it was to broadcast homosexual critique into the gay interstice of a pun."[44] Made lustrous now by all the muted lighting of indeterminacy, homosexual desire cannot be contained for the very reason that it cannot be confirmed: thus, for example, as much as Basil Hallward's arrested gaze falls short of grounds for any actual arrest, in Wilde's work no incident like it, that moment when someone can't stop looking at another no matter what the risk, can ever be definitively removed from the shadow of the doubt that falls on his. Take the gaze fixed on Salome—"How beautiful is the Princess Salome tonight!"[45]—how to avoid, anymore than the breathless young Syrian can the vision of grace that holds him, the wild surmise that the eye that loiters

[42] *Dorian Gray*, p. 15.

[43] D. A. Miller, "Anal Rope," *Representations* 32 (Fall 1990) (Berkeley: University of California Press), p. 119.

[44] Christopher Craft, "Alias Bunbury: Desire and Termination in *The Importance of Being Earnest*," in *Another Kind of Love: Male Homosexual Desire in English Discourse, 1850–1920* (Berkeley: University of California Press, 1994), p. 4. See also Jonathan Dollimore, *Sexual Dissidence: Augustine to Wilde, Freud to Foucault* (Oxford: Oxford University Press, 1991). For an especially precise and persuasive reading of the association of indeterminacy and sexuality in Wilde, see William A. Cohen, "Indeterminate Wilde," in *Sex Scandal* (Durham: Duke University Press, 1996).

[45] Oscar Wilde, *Salome* (1894), in *Major Works*, p. 302.

here—like the one taken with the spectacle of Juliet until she steps off the stage and too near the nuptial bar: " 'When is she Sybil Vane?'/ 'Never' "—is somehow the very same as the one whose homosexual desire is never quite named? In this way, the helplessness of the homosexual to determine the form and expression of his desire is avenged by the echo of his helplessness in the audience who hears—or is it hallucinates?—it.

Cold comfort though for the "exposed" heart that the "shallow prying eyes" who see him are no more able to decide how to receive it than he is how to present it. The multivalence of this involuntary spectacle does nothing to repair the fact that the figure whom it spotlights has no say over its production, and whose artistic powers of self-expression are paralyzed by the spell of the erotic, a sight "fascinating" enough to "absorb" his "whole nature, [his] whole soul, [his] very art itself."[46] The work of art is thus obliged to go elsewhere: the subject stripped of all his powers in the field of desire, which Hellenism had instructed him to make a thing of beauty, retreats from that field where he is compelled to concede defeat before the first shot, to a separate sphere, where, fueled by the energy of compensation, he redoubles the efforts of his will to cultivate the sense of self-mastery. Thus a paragraph in *The Picture of Dorian Gray* that places the hero on the waterfront, where he is seen, or almost, Bunburying with the gloves off—"moments . . . at night, when . . . in the sordid room of the little ill-famed tavern near the Docks, which under an assumed name, and in disguise, it was his habit to frequent"; "moments" of "mad hungers that grew more ravenous as he fed them"—is closely followed by a vision of the connoisseur whose orchestrated tastes are the very form of his own one art:

> Yet he was not really reckless, at any rate in his relations to Society. Once or twice every month during the winter, and on each Wednesday evening while the season lasted, he would throw open to the world his beautiful house and have the most celebrated musicians of the day to charm his guests with the wonders of their art. His little dinners, in the settling of which Lord Henry always assisted him, were noted as much for the careful selection and placing of those invited, as for the exquisite taste shown in the decoration of the table,

[46] *Dorian Gray*, pp. 11, 15.

23

with its subtle symphonic arrangements of exotic flowers, and embroidered cloths, and antique plate of gold and silver. Indeed, there were many who saw, or fancied that they saw, in Dorian Gray the true realization of a type of which they had often dreamed in Eton or Oxford days, a type that was to combine something of the real culture of the scholar with all the grace and distinction and perfect manner of a citizen of the world. To them he seemed to be of the company of those whom Dante describes as having sought to make themselves perfect by the worship of beauty.[47]

Small wonder, given the lingering odor of the waterfront that clings to him—"For while he fascinated many, there were not a few who distrusted him. . . . Curious stories became current about him . . . he had been seen brawling with foreign sailors"[48]—that his author would, with all the intentions of the artist, prepare Dorian Gray to face the society that wouldn't know what to make of the odor, or wouldn't know not to make too much. It is no surprise that in the book filled with the threat of social extermination that arises from uncontrollable desire, the work of art that can no longer take passion for its subject should take shape instead as the artfulness of a social being who knows better than to get caught with his pants down amongst his "mad hungers," preferring to exhibit for the consumption of society the more admirable tastes of the connoisseur; no surprise that a character so pressed would know how to translate the worship of beauty, which in Wilde's book—the passage is nowhere to be found in Dante's—is the grammar of ascent in the classic project of self-perfection into an aesthetic of social appearance. The portrait of the artist in *The Picture of Dorian Gray* is that of a young aesthete who takes for his medium the beau monde that Simmel calls the "art form of society," "the impersonal freedom of a mask,"[49] rather than those desires over which he has no artistic control in any case and which would land him in a state of exile as far removed from the graces of the brilliant company he keeps here as the coldest depths of Hell from the bright lights of the divinest comedy.

As this passage indicates, the armies of the will, after they lose the field of desire, do not restrict their exercises to the forces of reserve that would simply mask what they cannot control. A losing proposition anyway:

[47] Ibid. p. 100.
[48] Ibid. p. 110.
[49] Simmel, "Sociability," p. 46.

as we already have sufficient grounds to appreciate, no poise in the world could be worldly enough to master a language of desire that quite circumvents the subject's own mechanisms of consent or consciousness, the language of desire that, in Freud's own phrase, annuls the hold of the ego over his own house,[50] the language of desire that gives the color element to the picture of Dorian Gray—"sin is the only color element left in the modern world"—the picture that leaves him as exposed as the woman who walks the streets not far from his own stately home: "Yet he was afraid. Sometimes when he was down at his great house . . . entertaining the fashionable young men of his own rank who were his chief companions . . . he would suddenly leave his guests and rush back to town to see that the door had not been tampered with, and that the picture was still there. What if it should be stolen? The mere thought made him cold with horror. Surely the world would know his secret then. Perhaps the world already suspected it."[51]

The subject, powerless to conceal, or to choose how he reveals, the passions that course through him, a subject pitiful for all his fear even at his most enfranchised—and how much more so in the vivid abjection she is elsewhere cast—"You don't know what it is . . . to be . . . afraid every moment lest the mask be stripped from one's face"—rises to heroic versions of self-stylization, what Simmel's keenest heir called the presentation of the self in everyday life.[52] Making aesthetic virtue of social necessity, this subject manages not only to meet the expectations of propriety, but to welcome them with open arms; not merely to avoid the exile or imprisonment that is the fate of those who, by the practice of their bodily proclivities, violate social law, but the softer extermination that is the fate of those who, by virtue of their bodily defects, fail to make the social scene. Like the exhausted or terrified soul who knows to redouble the labors of gladness before those who expect nothing less, the grace of what we will call the "social body beautiful" is the finest development of the subject trained to feel a social demand as relentless as any law of gravity or psychic agency.

[50] "[T]he ego . . . is not even master in its own house"; Lecture XVIII in Freud, *Introductory Lectures*, p. 285.

[51] *Dorian Gray*, p. 110.

[52] Erving Goffman, *The Presentation of Self in Everyday Life* (New York: Anchor Books, 1959). See also Goffman's remarks on "passing" in *Stigma: Notes on the Management of Spoiled Identity* (New York: Simon & Schuster, 1963), pp. 73–90.

The Taming of Desire

"I must confess that I am much more interested in problems about techniques of the self and things like that than sex . . . sex is boring."[53] No less striking than the proposition itself, that *sex*, rather than this or that easily, or best forgotten, encounter, is boring, is the subject that he prefers instead: "techniques of the self and things like that." Once again, in other words, "those intentional and voluntary actions by which men not only set themselves rules of conduct, but also seek to transform themselves, to change themselves in their singular being, and to make their life into an oeuvre that carries certain aesthetic values and meets certain stylistic criteria."[54] Striking, to say the least, Foucault's sense that sex ceases to be interesting once it spins out of the orbit of our will, this settled preference for the subject of intentionality over the erotic drama of its decline, since, for "We Other Victorians," what compels us about sex is what compels us about it. For those of us who dwell in the shadow of the regime whose dimensions Foucault takes, whose laws Freud was busy codifying as science at the same time that its most fantastic aspects were told in the supernatural tales of libidinal horror no less exciting now than they were at the end of the last century, when they had their debut—including of

---

[53] "On the Genealogy of Ethics," in Foucault, *Ethics*, p. 253. Here I want to remark upon a difference between my own sense of the relation between the sexual and the volitional in Foucault's study of the ancients and that of David Halperin. In Halperin's reading of Foucault, the volitional character of the ancient project that animates the last two volumes of *The History of Sexuality* is quite consonant with his conception of the erotic. I think that Foucault's vision of "those intentional and voluntary actions" by which individuals and collectives "not only set themselves rules of conduct, but also seek to transform themselves" is purchased at the expense of the erotic, which is the ground where the will of the individual or the collective is annulled. There is a difference between the styles of life that are defined in relation to powers of sexual desire and discharge, and those powers themselves, and Foucault was interested in the first of these and not the second. This preference is apparent not only in his off-hand remark about his boredom with sex, but also in his Introduction to the second volume of *The History*. See Halperin, "The Queer Politics of Michel Foucault," in *Saint Foucault*, pp. 15–125; and his *One Hundred Years of Homosexuality and Other Essays on Greek Love*, (New York: Routledge, 1990). See also Joel Black, "Taking the Sex Out of Sexuality: Foucault's Failed History," in *Rethinking Sexuality: Foucault and Classical Antiquity*, edited by David H. J. Lamour, Paul Allen Miller, and Charles Platter (Princeton: Princeton University Press, 1998), pp. 42–60.

[54] Foucault, *Uses of Pleasure*, pp. 10–11.

course those written and lived by Wilde himself—in which forces of desire
make slaves of their subjects, the melodrama whose apparently eternal afterlife is available in mass cultural redactions ranging from the scary movie
where the dark places to which characters are led by their sexual desires is
matched by the force of the drive that leads them there, to the popular
contemporary cult that arraigns all matter of attraction as so many manners of addiction.[55]

Anyone who knows the first thing about him knows that Wilde
was no stranger to the thrill that Foucault claimed to have gotten over, no
one less so, and yet this character whose desires in the life, in the art, were
so famously out of his hands was attracted to the same ancient light that
the great philosopher hailed in the end. As well as he told the story about
the slave of love, and no version better than the one about the high-roller
whose life was "staked on a passion," Wilde was attracted nonetheless—
who isn't?—to the possibility of avoiding the damages done to the self by
passions, hungers, needs quite out one's control. The final three chapters
of this book seek to unearth elements of Wilde's schemes to reckon with
this contradiction by his usual method of having it both ways: schemes,
stoic and self-indulgent, to amend a law of desire grown powerful enough
to count by modern calculations as absolute; to perform, but also to ameliorate, the melodrama of the mortified will; to offset, or, more often, altogether remove its tragic tone; the last three chapters of this book seek to
reconstruct the paths by which Wilde strove to be as near as he could to
touching, in an age too late to grasp it, the fruit of his Hellenic ideal.

Such schemes involve not the seizing of desire but rather a vision
of its softening, not a subject strong enough to control his passions, but
rather species of passion that, by their very nature, are slight enough to be
as good as managed. Modest by Wilde's standards, such schemes imagine

---

[55] In "Epidemics of the Will," Eve Kosofsky Sedgwick describes the Manichaean drama
in which the absolute power of the will comes to grief at the hands of an even more absolute
power of desire. Sedgwick renders explicit the confusion of what attracts and what compels
and traces the career of this condensation from the dream-like fantasies of the fin de siècle
to the feet-on-the-ground panegyrics of contemporary self-help sensibilities. I am glad to
express my gratitude to Sedgwick for taking the dimensions of the donnée where from the
drama that I seek to study begins; for provoking my sense of the tyranny of desire that Wilde
devotes so much moxie to evade, counteract and ameliorate. See her *Tendencies* (Durham:
Duke University Press, 1993), p. 130–142.

no radical realignment that would put the subject back in the driver's seat of desire, but rather program the engine for a landing as soft as the ones brought about in *Earnest*, the sudden death, explosion and disappearance—all in good fun—of the various distractions to the marriage-plot orchestrated by characters who are themselves enough orchestrated by that plot to drop even their "irresistible attractions" if they ever actually get in its way. Leaving behind the athletic rigors of the ancients, Wilde gathers nearer a more recent plan for managing the drives, finely illustrated by a train of thought in political theory definitively described by Albert O. Hirschman in *The Passions and the Interests: Political Arguments for Capitalism Before its Triumph*, a train of thought which by an "astounding" change of mind over the course of many centuries ceased to condemn and came instead to approbate the love of monetary gain as a gentle motive, whose sweet temperament—Hirschman: "There was much talk, from the late seventeenth century on, about the *douceur* of commerce"—would counteract and calm other more ferocious hungers.[56]

The softer strains of passion that Wilde envisions, as we will have occasion to appreciate, at times bear a more than passing resemblance to "the *douceur* of commerce," a concept that accommodates not only the paleness of monetary interest, but also the polish of a cultivated detachment that knows to never value anyone as if he were the only one. But if the milder strains of passion in Wilde's book draw from the economic sentiments of an earlier century, the menace that is thus avoided, the threat attached to those that the softer ones are slated to supplant, is not exactly what the original framers of this psychological constitution had in mind, where the violence to be contained threatens first and foremost

---

[56] Albert O. Hirschman, *The Passions and the Interests: Political Arguments for Capitalism Before its Triumph* (Princeton: Princeton University Press, 1977), pp. 11, 59. For a depressing coda to the conception of economic interest as a calm and calming passion, see the conclusion to Max Weber's *The Protestant Ethic and the Spirit of Capitalism*, where he remarks its transformation into another form of drive: "In Baxter's view the care for external goods should only lie on the shoulders of the 'saint like a light cloak, which can be thrown aside at any moment.' But fate decreed that the cloak should become an iron cage." According to Weber's influential history, the irresistible urge for acquisition thus merges with the compelling passions they were once slated to contain and counteract. See his *The Protestant Ethic and The Spirit of Capitalism*, translated by Talcott Parsons (Los Angeles: Roxbury Publications, 1995), p. 181. Subsequent citations of this text refer to this edition.

the social order. The scheme of sublimation that Hirschman studies was concerned to defend that order, much like the celebrated symmetry of the Constitution in which this balance of powers, transposed from individual psyche to social polity, is writ large. For Wilde, on the other hand, whose sole interest in social schemes consisted in their value as a means by which the individual might be released from bothering about social schemes altogether—"The chief advantage that would result from the establishment of Socialism is, undoubtedly, the fact that Socialism would relieve us from that sordid necessity of living for others"[57]—the clear and present danger posed by the corrosive effects of desire has everything to do with the marring of the self rather than the upsetting of society, unless, of course, if the second brings about, say in the form of a stretch in prison, the first.

Or the terrors of starvation: one of the appetites that is displaced by a softer one is so fearful that the anxieties that attend sexual desire can feel comforting by comparison to it, the appetite of appetite itself. Except for a few letters from prison, a fairy tale or two, a passing joke about a pressing need for cucumber sandwiches or tea cake, hunger is mentioned in his writing hardly at all. Why would it be? And yet like all sorts of barely mentioned things, the fear of starvation is deep at the heart's core in Wilde; it is central to the exodus story this book aims to reconstruct, the passing from forms of wanting that cannot be borne to those that, even when they bear signs of doom, can be sustained with élan, even pleasure; after all, even those drawn to feast with panthers are bound to be better off than those with nothing to eat at all, the "great many people . . . always on the brink of sheer starvation."[58] Like the vengeful brother in *Dorian Gray*, who appears, as if from out of nowhere, to spoil the perfect life, or the debt collector expurgated from *Earnest*, the specter of starvation casts its shadow on Wilde's work, or, more exactly, the work of idleness that he recommends, the "doing nothing" whose "importance" he labors so warmly to assert.[59] It is as if the author had been suddenly called home to a hungry nation from the happy country he preferred, the utopia of indolence where, relieved of duty, men and women

[57] "The Soul of Man," p. 1.
[58] Ibid., p. 3.
[59] "The Critic as Artist," in *Critical Writings*, pp. 341–407.

might do what they want and therefore what matters; as if for all his ingenious devices to escape it, Wilde is harrowed by the ghost of a Protestant ethic, one that Weber describes—"even the wealthy shall not eat without working"—a puritanism whose arm proves long enough to arraign him after all.[60]

Less virulent than the hunger that leads to starvation are strains of desire that bring consequences no less dire in their own way. The attraction exerted by a charismatic figure, the attraction powerful enough to arrest the heart and the eye of those who admire him, an attraction that renders that subject helpless to look away vulnerable to the range of penalties reserved for those caught looking, from the mild but decisive discipline of the knowing, belligerent, or discomfited counterglance to more severe modes of mortification. These are passions impossible to disentangle from the homosexual. It goes without saying by now, I think, that, just as in his life, after its stop in Reading Gaol, Wilde could never have hoped to extricate himself from the subject charged with them, the feelings that he writes of in a novel used to make those charges stick could never dwell far from the species of yearning to which he gave up his name. For reasons that hardly require repeating here, this confusion of clandestine and dominant cultures of desire has been spun by interested parties to affirm the persistence of the homosexual in enemy territory, the nimble acts of circumlocution by which a kind of survival is accomplished, a survival no less miraculous, more so, really, considering all the breathtaking self-denial and deformation that is part of the package. It is time now to ponder briefly the obvious corollary—since what is not homosexual can never be rid of what is, therefore what is homosexual desire can never be rid of what is not—timely to ponder this, if only to recall that homosexual desire in Wilde, like sexual desire in general, is mingled with affairs that are in themselves quite removed from the dramas of the erotic.

If, as Miss Prism remarks when she instructs her charge to omit the chapter of her Political Economy given over to the Fall of the Rupee, "it is somewhat too sensational. . . .Even these metallic problems have their melodramatic side,"[61] it stands to reason that the problems of even the

[60] Weber, *The Protestant Ethic*, p. 159.
[61] *Earnest*, p. 502.

most melodramatic sensation are themselves indexed to the conditions of currency. If these melodramatic sensations are never more pressing than when no image of them is present, the strains of the dismal science make themselves felt in the midst even of the most thrilling passions. Thus even where the desire in question bears the unmistakable signature of the male homosexual—"It was such love as Michael Angelo had known, and Montaigne, and Winckelmann, and Shakespeare himself"[62]—such amatory tenderness,[63] as much as it might discomfit a regime of heterosexual masculinity, impinges as well on the push and shove of an economy based on a tender not amatory, but legal, a market economy whose turnover demand has as little time for eternal devotion as space for the eternal object that would merit it: "[I]t was really love—[it] had nothing in it that was not noble and intellectual. It was not that mere physical admiration of beauty that is borne of the senses, and that dies when the senses tire."[64] Such persistent desire runs counter to the imperatives of consumption that came to be regarded as critical by the late nineteenth century, when, at least according to the prevailing school of neoclassicism,[65] scarce supply had given way to insufficient demand as the specter that haunted the economy, and when, in Simmel's words, "the seller" was obliged "to call forth new and differentiated needs."[66] The noble love that "Michael Angelo had known, and Montaigne, and Winckelmann, and Shakespeare himself" is a risible atavism by the calculations of the sophisticated aesthete whose spirit covers so much of Wilde's novel. It is an adolescent idealism by the calculation that reduces all passionate investments to the common denominator

[62] *Dorian Gray*, p. 136.

[63] The phrase is from *The Times* is review of *In Memoriam* (quoted in Christopher Ricks, *Tennyson* [New York: Macmillan, 1972], p. 219). See also Benjamin Jowett's remark that Tennyson's affection for Shakespeare's sonnets stopped just short of an alarming "sympathy with Hellenism"(quoted by Ricks, p. 215).

[64] *Dorian Gray*, p. 93.

[65] See Lawrence Birken, *Consuming Desire: Sexual Science and the Emergence of a Culture of Abundance 1871–1914* (Ithaca: Cornell University Press, 1988). See also Regenia Gagnier, *The Insatiability of Human Wants: Economics and Aesthetics in Market Society* (Chicago: University of Chicago Press, 2000); for an account of Wilde that places him generally in a critical relation to market capitalism while also engaging its forms, see Regenia Gagnier, *Idylls of the Marketplace: Oscar Wilde and the Victorian Marketplace* (Stanford: Stanford University Press, 1986).

[66] Georg Simmel, "The Metropolis and Mental Life," in *Sociology*, p. 420.

of their inevitable and ultimate expenditure—"the only difference between a caprice and a life long romance is that a caprice lasts a little longer,"[67] and no less out of place in the rush of up-market commodity consumption that occupies as much of its plot as any more transgressive desire.

The fit between the economic and erotic elements of Wilde's project is as fine as can be. Like the docile bodies and the investments of faith that sponsor, and are in turn sponsored by, the operations of capitalism, the lighter brands of desire that Wilde labors to produce not only work to serve the demands of market society, they also take their forms from its material.[68] Thus, for example, what Simmel calls the philosophy of money dwells at the heart of the urbane passion that displaces the tyrannical magnetism of the charismatic spectacle: the cosmopolitan eye that knows better than fix itself on any single person, but rather loves the entire expanse of the social horizon; the devotion of the aesthete, whose vision of art is a comprehensive history of all the passionate attitudes in the world, attitudes glamorous enough to attract us both as an infinite company of models and objects for our own; the turn-on-a-dime impermanence of the one-night stand, the transitory states of interest in an other that leave us ready for countless more; the scrutiny of the social scientist that dwells near the aesthete's in more books than those of Wilde, the eye whose attraction to this or that personal instance is always the means of lighting the way to the vision of society that he loves more dearly.

Such society, the one that Simmel appreciated as its art form— "Sociability is the game in which one 'does as if' all were equal, and at the same time, as if one honored each of them in particular. And to 'do as if' is no more a lie than play or art are lies because of their deviation from reality"[69]—is the flower of the market culture he describes in *The Philosophy of Money*:

> While at an earlier stage man paid for the smaller number of his dependencies
> with the narrowness of personal relations, often with their personal irreplace-
> ability, we are compensated for the great quantity of our dependencies by the

[67] *Dorian Gray*, p. 24.

[68] Michel Foucault, *Discipline and Punish* (New York: Pantheon, 1977); See also Weber, *The Protestant Ethic*.

[69] Simmel, "Sociability," p. 49.

indifference towards the respective persons and by our liberty to change them at will. And even though we are much more dependent on the whole of society through the complexity of our needs on the one hand, and the specialization of our abilities on the other, than are primitive people who could make their way through life with their very narrow group, we are remarkably independent of every specific member of this society.[70]

A greater care for society as a whole, an ultimate indifference toward any individual; this "peculiar leveling of emotional life that is ascribed to contemporary times" has aspects as various as the two pictures of Dorian Gray. There is, on one side, "the ease of intellectual understanding which exists even between people of the most divergent natures and positions;" the elegant international style of thought, the moral elegance that Wilde hails as "the cosmopolitanism of the future."[71] On the other hand, there is the "blasé attitude," the final finding of a worldview dominated entirely by a money economy, where all differences in quality have been reduced to differences in quantity:

> Whereas the cynic is still moved to a reaction by the sphere of value, even if in the perverse sense that he considers the downward movement of values part of the attraction of life, the blasé person . . . has completely lost the feeling for value differences. He experiences all things as being of an equally dull and gray hue, as not worth getting excited about, particularly where the will is concerned.[72]

How wonderful is this world as Wilde sees it, though; all the wonder of the visible world rather than a single "dull gray hue," a gorgeous spectrum in which each episode of color is all the richer for the fact that, at the end of the day, or the night, or the briefest glance, it finally fades into the light

[70] Simmel, *The Philosophy of Money*, p. 298. See also Durkheim, *Division of Labor*.

[71] Ibid., p. 432. See Wilde, "The Critic as Artist," p. 294. On the complex structure of detachment in and beyond Wilde, see Amanda Anderson, *The Powers of Distance: Cosmopolitanism and the Cultivation of Detachment.* (Princeton: Princeton University Press, 2001). Anderson's account of the category of detachment, and of the correlative character of the cosmopolitan, has helped me to understand elements of light desire that I would have been otherwise disposed not to see. It isn't feasible for me to explicate those things here, except to say that I must credit Anderson with prompting me to recognize these desires as positive virtues as much as they are defensive ruses.

[72] Simmel, *The Philosophy of Money*, p. 256.

of commonness, no more than an instance, a single showing of the social mosaic. Like the art form of society that Simmel himself so brilliantly illuminates, the party (*gesellschaft*) that makes the pedestrian fiction of equality that is the most ordinary assumption of market society (*gesellschaft*) into a form of grace, the act of discernment accomplished by the fine eye of Wilde's cosmopolitan delivers that society from a dullness worse than death. And if this vision of urbanity raises the world that it sees from the depression endemic to the philosophy of money, it is indebted in turn to that blasé attitude for providing the model by which it may fashion itself as a mode of interest that cures by displacing the terror of the arrested eye. If the joyful vision of the *flâneur* is more excited than the dull one trained on the monotony of market values, it is calmer than the eye so compelled by the sight of the charismatic figure who seems to draw within his single person all that is attractive about people in general, the eye so compelled that it cannot turn away to save its life.

But it is the investments of art rather than money, aesthetics and not economics, upon which Wilde's project most depends. There is no more prominent or pervasive source and paradigm for light, lightened desires than the experience of the aesthetic as Wilde takes it up.[73] "Art does not hurt us," he famously declares: "The tears we shed at a play are a type of the exquisite sterile emotions that it is the function of Art to awaken. We weep but we are not wounded. . . . It is through Art and Art only . . . that we can shield ourselves from the sordid perils of actual existence"[74]—sordid perils, such as those represented by the sudden appearance of the police. Beneath the elevated regions of disinterestedness, there is the prosaic stratagem practiced by the figure of the painter in *The Picture of Dorian Gray* and by Wilde himself in Old Bailey, the basic ruse by which passion is defined as a work of art in the hopes of escaping prosecution for it. We hear this claim of aesthetic immunity in Lord Henry's

---

[73] As we will see, Wilde borrows and bends the conception of the aesthetic promulgated most significantly by Kant. See Immanuel Kant, *The Critique of Judgment*, translated with Analytical Indexes by James Creed Meredith (Oxford: Oxford University Press, 1952). See also Adam Smith, *The Theory of Moral Sentiments, or, An Essay Towards an Analysis of the Principles by Which Men Naturally Judge Concerning the Conduct and Character, First of Their Neighbors, and Afterwards of Themselves* (Edinburgh : Printed by J. Hay & Co. for W. Creech, 1813).

[74] "The Critic as Artist," p. 274.

final confession, or rather, by what is excluded from it. "Life is not governed by will or intention. Life is a question of nerves and fibres, and slowly built-up cells in which thought hides itself and passion has its dreams." The thought of what inhabits these cells may put us in mind of a dormant malignancy suddenly spelled out one fine day in a positive diagnosis, or, related to that, but surely closer to the doom on Wilde's own mind, the image of the author himself, the one who a few years later came to occupy cell C. 3.3. during his sentence of hard labor for passions that he felt unable to contain. Before that one, though, Lord Henry's sentence sounds the depths discovered in a portrait of a lady definitively appreciated by his famous teacher: "The presence that rose thus so strangely beside the waters, is expressive of what in the ways of a thousand years men had come to desire. Hers is the head upon which all 'the ends of the world are come,' and the eyelids are a little weary. It is a beauty wrought out from within upon the flesh, the deposit, cell by cell, of strange thoughts and fantastic reveries and exquisite passions."[75]

The sordid perils of existence from which art shields us extend beyond those embodied in a figure of the law. In Wilde's book, they include as well those of embodiment itself. By his lights, the disinterestedness of aesthetic interest is a matter of its abstractness; by his rendering, the realm of need from which Kant's canonical account detaches the aesthetic becomes a bodily need in particular, and a particular bodily need—the one that ends in starvation. And in his story of aesthetic salvation, those who dwell under the shadow of starvation as punishment for their indolence are led away from worry as bodily appetite gives way to the "subtle susceptibilities," "wild ardours," and "impossible desires" instilled by the work of art, forms of borrowed passion that, whatever their terrors, are as distant from the prospect of famine as the pang of the heart that makes us know we're alive from the attack that makes us know we will not be for long.[76] On rare occasions, desire is shielded from the sordid perils of existence not by the resort to art, but rather a flight from it. Thus Wilde's theory of the boredom that alleviates a desire that mortifies its

---

[75] Walter Pater, *The Renaissance*, edited by Adam Phillips (Oxford: Oxford University Press, 1990), p. 80.
[76] "The Critic as Artist," p. 276.

subject by terminating it before the horror starts draws on the model of the "merely" sensuous passion, which, in contrast to the metaphysical achievements of its aesthetic counterpart, suffers the exhaustion that is the fate of all flesh. An exception that proves the rule: no doubt that the work of art is the brightest star of the light desires that Wilde heralds.

And the artist? We have encountered him already. He is the figure Wilde casts as the alien agent of desire, the devious aesthete who actually instills the impulses that he claims only to bring out—"You, Mr. Gray, you yourself, with your rose-red youth and your rose-white boyhood, you have had passions that have made you afraid, thoughts that have filled you with terror, day-dreams and sleeping dreams whose mere memory might stain your cheek with shame"—to free them and thus to free the boy himself: "Live! Live the wonderful life that is in you."[77] He is the better maker in Dorian Gray who, like the spirit of a subject named Power, manages to persuade us that the formula of our freedom is to call our own the sexuality it has implanted in us: "The irony of this deployment is in having us believe that our "liberation" is in the balance." Here is Wilde's portrait of the modern artist, whose medium, unlike that of his ancient ancestor, is the desires of another rather than his own:

> Talking to him was like playing upon an exquisite violin. He answered to every touch a thrill of the bow. . . . There was something terribly enthralling in the exercise of influence. . . . To project one's soul into some gracious form, and let it tarry there for a moment . . . to convey one's temperament into another as though it were a subtle fluid or strange perfume. . . . He was a marvelous type, too, this lad . . . or could be fashioned into a marvelous type, at any rate. Grace was his, and the white purity of boyhood, and beauty such as old Greek marbles kept for us. There was nothing that one could not do with him. He could be made a Titan or a toy.[78]

Lord Henry delighting behind the scenes at his knack for imposing the temperament that he claims only to observe, to form the subject whose self-determination is all he claims to care about, confirms a most paranoid vision of power, and a most appreciative one, as well. If this sight puts us

[77] *Dorian Gray,* p. 23.
[78] Ibid., pp. 33–34.

in mind, say, of a suspicion about the work of modern psychotherapy that begins with Karl Kraus's bitter hunch—"psychoanalysis is the illness for which it claims to be the cure"—and continues with Foucault's full-scale prosecution, it puts us in mind, as well—more so, really—of the classic work of art: "To a large extent the lad was really his own creation."[79]

Exit the hero of desire hailed as the artist of himself, "a subject . . . distinguished by his ability to subdue the tumultuous forces that were loosed within him, to stay in control of his store of energy, and to make his life into an oeuvre," vanished now "those intentional and voluntary actions by which men not only set themselves rules of conduct, but also seek to transform themselves, to change themselves in their singular being, and to make their life into an oeuvre that carries certain aesthetic values and meets certain stylistic criteria." And in their place a new kind of artist, the one who insinuates foreign desires in a now passive subject, a figure called by many names in Wilde—"It comes to us, this terrible shadow, with many gifts in its hands. . . . And so it is not our own life that we live, but the lives of the dead, and the soul that dwells within us is no single spiritual entity, making us personal and individual. . . . It fills us with impossible desires, and makes us follow what we know we cannot gain"[80]—but whom we know full well as the subject of homosexual seduction, most candid in the closet where Dorian Gray observes with "real pleasure" as the picture takes on the "moods and passions" that he projects there, "atom calling to atom in secret love or strange affinity."[81]

The deep character who makes the desires of others his own work of art will be familiar to those schooled in contemporary theory, and in particular the concept of power that makes its debut in Foucault's incalculably influential introduction to *The History of Sexuality*, the concept of power that makes a grim epilogue to the ancient adventure that he studies in the volumes that follow, a sad ending in which the management of desire ("the ability to control, limit, and apportion it in the right manner") has been confiscated by a modern regime as cunning as any in the history of the world. A force whose capacity to control the course of desire

---

[79] Ibid., p. 49.
[80] "The Critic as Artist," p. 276.
[81] *Dorian Gray*, p. 127.

in the subject that it thus governs mirrors and magnifies the grasp on his passions that the ancients sought to arrange for the subject himself: the hand that takes up the ancient scepter of desire is as sure as its ancestor's, but it is suppler now. Skilled in the classic style to manipulate its form and expression, its reach now extends further by a distance made familiar to us by the measure of the postmodernism disseminated in no small part through the very offices of Foucault's concept of power itself. While the ancient arts of sexual self-management confront the erotic desires they seek to place under their command, the flexuous forms of modern power that Foucault anatomizes constructs them: the censorship that incites what it officially prohibits, the interrogation that calls forth what it seeks out, the science that implants the perversions that it defines.

It's no surprise if, as I think, this modern agency is the alienated majesty of the ancient self as Foucault would have it, that it has been so routinely arraigned, despite the author's repeated denials, as the ghost of a subject in the poststructuralist machine, an infinitely ingenious and malevolent agent, at home in a Hegelian conspiracy theory, but quite unfit for a model of social determination, which, like its cognates in the sphere of language and psyche, claims to have done with the subject once and for all. And no wonder, then, that those practices that the ancients in Foucault's history assign the self to manage his own desires should bear such a striking resemblance to the tactics by which modern power came to manage it for him: the labor of constant inspection, first and foremost, stretching from the institution of confession to the sciences of sexology, a labor guided and fueled by a regulative principle of abstinence or nor-mality, much as the self-accountings of asceticism get their wary eye for the least sign and the most hidden form of erotic yearning from the ideal of chastity that they putatively seek to enforce. No wonder that the policy of power toward the desire that it "harried"[82] looks as much like that of the hedonist who aims to tune and refine his own pleasures—Alexander Nehamas: "The purpose of these complex exercises [is] . . . not only the repression of pleasure, it is the regulation of pleasure. Its objective is not denial, it is satisfaction."[83]—as the silent eye of supervision that is trained

---

[82] Foucault, *The History of Sexuality: Volume I*, p. 45.
[83] Alexander Nehamas, "Subject and Abject," *The New Republic*, 15 February 1993, p. 35.

on the pleasures of others: "Power operated as a mechanism of attraction; it drew out those peculiarities over which it kept watch. Pleasure spread to the power that harried it; power anchored the pleasure it uncovered . . . *perpetual spirals of power and pleasure*."[84] And no surprise if their origin is the war within that Foucault's ancients envision as the model of self-management—to struggle against "the desires and the pleasure" was to cross swords with oneself—that modern power should draw so close to the desire it regulates, that their commerce with one another should involve "not boundaries to be crossed, but *perpetual spirals of power and pleasure*." No surprise that Foucault, despite his denials and despite the fact that neither the force of logic nor the evidence of history obliged him to do so, stresses the consolidation of power in his analysis of the game (rather say, than the competence of resistance, or both), since this stress echoes, only in a note turned tragic now, the strength that the ancient self gathers to himself in the battle with his desires.

And no wonder then, that Foucault's model of modern power has leant itself so graciously to aesthetic appreciation in the years since he published it, that his introduction to the *History of Sexuality* should have inspired a movement in criticism that has, in the subtlest measures of those forms, seen all the charm of art.[85] No wonder, if the social forms that, by the lights of this criticism, are illuminated and even comprehended by aesthetic ones should be haunted, like the constellation of stars that projects the outline of the lone warrior, by the work performed by the hero of desire imagined by his ancients, the constant exercises of self-control through which he labored to be beautiful.[86] The portrait of the artist that

[84] *History of Sexuality: Volume I.*, p. 45 (emphasis in original).

[85] Founding examples of this school of criticism include D. A. Miller, *The Novel and the Police* (Berkeley: University of California Press, 1988); and Stephen Greenblatt, *Shakespearian Negotiations: The Circulation of Social Energy in Renaissance England* (Berkeley: University of California Press, 1988). For the spirit of power that subtends the aesthetic view of domination in recent criticism, see also Foucault, *Discipline and Punish*.

[86] No wonder as well that the most arresting criticism leveled against the way Foucault tells the ancient adventure of self-cultivation should take issue, first of all, with his disinclination to consider the external standards that, at least according to the scholar who started him on the subject, gives direction to this adventure. "It is quite true," Pierre Hadot remarks, "that . . . the ancients did speak of an 'art of living.' It seems to me, however, that the description M. Foucault gives of what I had termed 'spiritual exercises,' and which he prefers to call 'techniques of the self,' is precisely focused far too much on the 'self,' or at

Foucault apprehends in the ancient practices of self-regulation has its shadowy afterlife—or is it the other way around?—in the picture he takes of the power behind these modern social forms, the power whose ambiguous undulations appear half of the time as the savoir faire of the finest hand. Never that of the King now—"we must imagine power without the king"—not any specifiable human being, of course, or even any specifiable social site where the instruments of domination are concentrated, but rather the ghost that arises from an ensemble of practices too dispersed to count as the property of this or that potentate, class, or social group.[87]

The resemblance though between these installations of desire in Wilde and Foucault illuminates a deep difference between these two, elsewhere so close, that allows us near the presence of the spirit that animates the whole of my story here. For while Foucault sees no reason to cheer the implantations of sexuality that he seeks to expose, little good to come from an erotic universe polluted by these fictions, unless and until they are expunged, Wilde celebrates them as the means by which we escape all the risk of the hungers we can do nothing to control. What Foucault dismisses as a diet of propaganda that keeps us from a richer feast—the party of "bodies and pleasures" liberated from the discursive impositions of power[88]—Wilde seizes as the golden ticket to a place at that blessed table where we can have our cake and eat it, too.

---

least on a specific conception of the self." For Hadot, Foucault declines to recognize that the self—"the best portion of the self"—whose cultivation the ancients sought to inculcate shapes itself to the contours of universal reason: "The 'best portion of oneself,' then, is, in the last analysis, a transcendent self. Seneca does not find his joy in 'Seneca,' but by transcending 'Seneca'; by discovering that there is within him—within all human beings, that is, and within the cosmos itself—a reason which is part of universal reason." What is the "specific self" that, by Hadot's lights, Foucault cares for too much but the microcosmic analogue to that familiar, indeed infamous, mode of power whose operations are quite indifferent to objective moral norms, except as an instrument of its own expansion? See Pierre Hadot, *Philosophy as a Way of Life: Spriritual Exercises from Socrates to Foucault*, edited with an Introduction by Arnold I. Davidson, translated by Michael Chase (Cambridge: Blackwell, 1996), pp. 206–7.

[87] Foucault, *History of Sexuality, Volume I.*, p. 91.

[88] Ibid., p. 159.

TWO

OSCAR WILDE IN JAPAN:
AESTHETICISM, ORIENTALISM, AND THE
DEREALIZATION OF THE HOMOSEXUAL

The story is simply this. . . . Two months ago I went to
a [party]. . . . after I had been in the room about ten
minutes, talking to . . . tedious Academicians, I suddenly became conscious that someone was looking at
me. I turned halfway round, and saw [him] for the first
time. When our eyes met, I felt that I was growing
pale. A curious sensation of terror came over me. I knew
that I had come face to face with someone whose mere
personality was so fascinating that, if I allowed it to do
so, it would absorb my whole nature, my whole soul, my
very art itself. I did not want any external influence in
my life. I have always been my own master; had at least
always been so, till I met [him]. . . . Then—but I don't
know how to explain it to you. Something seemed to
tell me that I was on the verge of a terrible crisis in my
life. I had a strange feeling that Fate had in store for
me exquisite joys and exquisite sorrows.
—Oscar Wilde, *The Picture of Dorian Gray*

FOR ALL OF ITS terror, the attraction confessed in this passage from
The Picture of Dorian Gray is common to us; the coerciveness that
characterizes desire in Wilde's telling of it, a coerciveness that, de-
feating initial efforts at containment—"if I allowed it to do so, it would
absorb my whole nature, my whole soul, my very art itself"—eventually
masters the subject it invades, makes his story difficult to distinguish from
one closer to home. If this passage sounds like the confession of a modern

41

homosexual, it's not because the man who admits his desire for another gains identity, but rather because he loses self-control. Whatever else separates the love featured in the contemporary coming-out story, where desire is taken as the signature of its subject, from the one pictured in Wilde's text, where it disperses rather than defines him, they are united by the power to compel. Conceptions of desire as different from one another as the centrifugal from the centripetal, as an aesthetic of impersonality from a politics of identity, share a conviction that the shape of our passions, no less than the place of our birth, or the source of our illness, is quite out of our hands. A fear of desire, powerful enough in late-nineteenth-century texts like *The Picture of Dorian Gray* and *Dr. Jekyl and Mr. Hyde* to become indistinguishable from desire itself, has its cause in its capacity to compromise the will of the subject confirmed or vaporized by it; a fear of desire no less hard at work in the late twentieth century than in the late nineteenth inhabits the common sense that what attracts coerces.

But however powerful the drive of desire may seem, the testimony of the merest whim will indicate that it's not pervasive. It is altogether absent, for example, in *The Importance of Being Earnest*, where the frightening passion that Wilde calls the enthralling effects of a young man in *Dorian Gray* is faded into the daylight of desires that, like the occasional cigarette, the weekend escapade, or the momentary reverie, are determined entirely by the subject who indulges them.

Such governance is administered by a variety of management styles in and beyond *The Importance of Being Earnest*, beginning with the familiar strategy of the double-life, well-outfitted here with false names and alibis. A tactic defined in the late nineteenth century by the difference between Dr. Jekyl and Mr. Hyde, between Dorian Gray and his portrait, and in the late twentieth by the difference between the wholesome heroine of the situation comedy, and her dark cousin, leaves the pursuit of pleasure to the discretion of its subject:

> You have invented a very useful younger brother called Ernest, in order that you may be able to come up to town as often as you like. I have invented an invaluable permanent invalid called Bunbury, in order that I may be able to go down into the country whenever I choose.[1]

[1] Oscar Wilde, *The Importance of Being Earnest* [1899], Act 1, in *Complete Plays* (London: Methuen, 1988), p. 224. All subsequent quotations of *Earnest* will refer to this edition and will be cited parenthetically.

But the manipulation of desire in Wilde's comedy exceeds what is normally accommodated by the double-life. The dandy that speaks in this passage is unusually modest in the account he furnishes of his modus operandi: the power he possesses over his wishes is more than the capacity to choose when he gives in to them; as half of the labor performed by the term "Bunbury"—a fiction that names both the "friend" who gives the pursuit of pleasure its excuse as well as the pleasure itself ("Bunbury-ing")—indicates, Algernon determines not only the timing of his capitulation to his wishes, but also their very character.

Comprehending everything from cradle to grave in *The Importance of Being Earnest*, where characters are commended or condemned for the conditions of their birth, the circumstances of their death, and the state of their health, the spirit of voluntarism is never more striking than when it casts "an irresistible fascination" as an act of caprice: "For me you have an irresistible fascination. . . . my ideal has always been to love someone of the name of Ernest."[2] This speech may put us in mind of the familiar testimony of the modern sexual subject, who might "respect" a member of the unpreferred gender, "might admire" his or her "character," but cannot offer "undivided attention,"[3] but a gap as wide as the gulf between free will and fate divides Wilde's character from the one inducted by a more recent discourse of desire. For despite the claim that her preference for the name of Ernest is irresistible, it is readily abandoned. In the rush to the altar that concludes *The Importance of Being Earnest*, we may forget that Cecily is content with a man whose name she had earlier declared would disqualify him as the object of her "undivided attention"; we may forget that for fully 50 percent of the "Ernestosexual" community, being Ernest proves not so important after all. Freed from any responsibility to an anterior condition that can be ignored or concealed, but hardly wished away, the subject of desire, like the masochist who knows the ropes better than the master who applies them, or a diarist whose record of events is a work of fantasy, paradoxically chooses what she cannot resist and is thus just as free, by means of a safe word or the sound of the wedding bell, to be released from it.

[2] *Earnest*, p. 229.
[3] Ibid., p. 259.

43

The light desire that governs *The Importance of Being Earnest* partakes of a late-Victorian climate of manufactured and manipulable passion associated with Wilde in particular, and Aestheticism in general. When Cecily describes the diary of her fictional devotion to Ernest as "a very young girl's record of her own thoughts and impressions, and consequently meant for publication,"[4] she embraces the exhibitionism that Gilbert and Sullivan, in their parody of the Aesthete's pretenses, arraign as Wilde's own most prominent feature. The character in *Patience* that everyone recognized as Aestheticism's self-styled spokesman confesses that his "languid love for lilies," "Lank limbs and haggard cheeks," "dirty greens," and "all one sees that's Japanese," is a sham affection, born of a morbid love of admiration![5]

And if the passion championed by Wilde in *The Importance of Being Earnest*, the pre—or extramarital proclivities contrived and controlled by the subject who entertains them, circulated more broadly in the culture of his day, other versions of it are rehearsed in our own. Wilde's brand of desire-lite will be both familiar and unfamiliar to those schooled in contemporary theories of dissident sexualities: familiar because of its egregious artificiality—cutting itself off from Nature where defenses of passions eccentric to the marriage plot, from Whitman's to those of recent gay essentialists, have found their grass-roots support. Asserting itself not as a fact of life, but rather as a work of art, such desire may put us in mind of the performances of gender and sexuality that recent theorists have celebrated.

It will also be familiar because of the optimism of the will that defines it. Carole Ann Tyler has argued that recent reviews of gender and sexual performance appeal to their actors intentions to separate theaters of insurrection from rituals of conformity:

> If all identities are alienated and fictional, then the distinction between parody, mimicry, or camp, and imitation, masquerade, or playing it straight is no longer self-evident. What makes the one credible and the other incredible

---

[4] Ibid., p. 256.

[5] William Gilbert and Arthur Sullivan, *Patience*, in *Complete Plays* (New York: Norton, 1976), p. 168.

when both are fictions? The answer, it seems, are the author's intentions: parody is legible in the drama of gender performance if someone meant to script it, intending it to be there.[6]

Wilde's light passion becomes unfamiliar, though, when we consider that this performance of desire works not to subvert heterosexual normativity, but rather to cooperate with it. Confined to the moment and from the materials of whimsy, the "irresistible attraction" to the name "Ernest" is abandoned when it proves discordant to the wedding march; the desires embodied in Bunbury are made to disappear like so much smoke at the first sound of wedding bells.

Dwelling all in fun and easily put aside before the altar, the airy passion of *The Importance of Being Earnest* is thrown into relief by the escalating anxiety about certain extramarital pleasures that defined Wilde's cultural situation, an escalating anxiety marked and arranged by the scandals and legislation that crowded the decades during which he wrote, culminating in the show trial where he found himself cast as the star witness for a love that he had spent considerable wit to avoid having to name. An acquired passion, less like an infectious disease than a love of the dance, the desire that, for all its lightness, moves more than the plot of *The Importance of Being Earnest* is no apology for dissident sexualities: it is rather an effort to prevent the need to make one.

To recognize that Wilde is never more a good citizen than when he flouts the conventions of referentiality is to notice again that social effects cannot be neatly collated with linguistic categories. But I want to suggest that the light passion that dwells on the surface of *The Importance of Being Earnest* does more to enhance our appreciation of the complexity of desire than encourage a by-now common apprehensiveness about certain poststructuralist efforts to align resistance to reference with resistance to the Law. I want to suggest that desire-lite, the domesticated passion that we have sampled in *The Importance of Being Earnest*, sometimes has a surprisingly foreign source; this house-brand of libido is often produced with foreign help.

[6] Carole-Anne Tyler, "Boys Will Be Girls: The Politics of Gay Drag," in *Inside/Out: Lesbian Theories, Gay Theories*, edited by Diana Fuss (New York: Routledge, 1991), p. 54.

Frantz Fanon, in his canonical account of the Western sexual imagination, describes an association of eros and exotic ethnicity more familiar than the one we will investigate here. Already active in the late nineteenth century, the association Fanon outlines has only intensified with the passing years: "One is no longer aware of the Negro, but only of a penis: the Negro is eclipsed. He is turned into a penis. He *is* a penis."[7] For all its raciness, the condensation the psychiatrist locates in the waking dreams of whites about blacks is as routine as a man in a polyester suit. Fanon's bold eye resolves the image of a cultural figure whose staying power has spanned several centuries, an image uncovered recently both by Robert Mapplethorpe's explicitness and by the often perfect integration of racial and sexual aversion that has attended it.

As its obtrusiveness in Mapplethorpe's photograph suggests, the threat of sexuality commonly embodied in the black man, as the black man, dwells in its undeniability; rendered vivid by the failure to cover it. While the artful passions featured in Wilde's comedy turn on a dime, or on a dictate of chapel and hearth, while "irresistible attractions" there disappear the instant they prove inconvenient to the regime of church and state, the desire in, and for what will not be contained by, the polyester suit is itself too compelling to respect the white-collar requirements of nine-to-five.

The field of color where appetites coercive enough to refuse the impressive demands of marriage plot or workplace extends beyond the skin tone recorded in the Mapplethorpe photograph. If the black man and black woman are typically cast as figures of a sexuality too compelling to be stopped by red lights, time clocks, or the check points of apartheid, other races, such as those who attend the opium den that Dorian Gray frequents, are attached to other, no less coercive strains of desire, cast either as their subject or object. Those addicted to what, in an irony of imperialism, was called a Chinese drug, "grotesque things that lay in . . . fantastic postures on the ragged mattresses" are themselves "crouching Malays," whose nationality, like the "odour of opium," is absorbed by the

[7] Frantz Fanon, *Black Skin, White Masks* (London: Paladin, 1970), p. 120 (emphasis in original).

den's clientele, generally: "A crooked smile, like a Malay crease, writhed across the face of one of the women."[8]

But if the dark compulsions clothed in the polyester suit of the black man, or housed in the opium den, are sometimes affiliated with exotic races, the desires that concern us here sometimes take their light from the land of the rising sun. In order to assess the labor done by the figure of Japan to promote safer passions, we need first to recall that this malleable desire is first and foremost a work of art. Whatever it isn't, the work of art is the domain of the artist's will. If art, according to Wilde's famous meditation, evades the constraints of mimesis, it is all the more the servant of the artist; if Wilde frees art from its bondage to accuracy, he makes it the compliant medium of the artist's will.

Wilde's account of the work of art recalls the child's play recorded by Freud, in which the infant masters what elsewhere masters him. "I don't want to be at the mercy of my emotions," Dorian Gray declares in a fit of pique, "I want to use them, to enjoy them, and to dominate them." Such power is achieved only when emotions, and desire chief among them, are spirited away from the element of blind compulsion that Wilde, in the following passage, calls "action:"

> There is no mode of action, no form of emotion, that we do not share with the lower animals. It is only by language that we rise above them, or above each other. [Action] is a blind thing dependent on external influences, and moved by an impulse of whose nature it is unconscious.[9]

If Wilde's account of "action" resembles our own ideas about the vicissitudes of sexuality, this is not only because of its animal and unconscious elements, but also, and most importantly, because it is driven by "external influences" and "impulse[s]." As much as anything else, Wilde's aversion to the outdoors, his distaste for the natural, is a dislike for the coercions of desire that he finds there. Only when desire migrates to the house of art does it acquire the pliancy necessary to render it safe for Christian law and family movie.

---

[8] Oscar Wilde, *The Picture of Dorian Gray*, edited by Donald Lawler (New York: Norton, 1988), pp. 224–25.

[9] "The Critic as Artist" (1891), in The *Artist as Critic: Critical Writings of Oscar Wilde*, edited by Richard Ellmann (Chicago: University of Chicago Press, 1968), p. 359.

In the figure of Japan, the artfulness of desire-lite finds agreeable surroundings. When, in their litany of Aesthetic tastes, Gilbert and Sullivan mention the "longing for all one sees that's Japanese," they refer to a style as central to the 1880s as the color black was to the 1980s. A part of a long line of fashions given over to the celebration of the artificial, the rage for things Japanese was as much as anything else a longing for an exoticism removed from the realm of the real. In an early instance of Japanese exceptionalism, the land of the rising sun, in contrast to the various regions of the non-Occidental world that imperial cartography mapped as a wildlife park, was apprehended by Western eyes as a palace of art. Starting with its "opening" to the West in the middle of the nineteenth century, Japan had become a storehouse for English, American, and French artists and collectors; the Impressionists, for example, located Japan as the home of their signature styles.

"Now, do you really imagine that the Japanese people, as they are presented to us in art, have any existence? If you do, you have never understood Japanese art at all," Wilde declares in a famous oriental travelogue sandwiched into "The Decay of Lying"—less a travelogue, really, than an explanation of why no such thing is necessary. "The Japanese people are the deliberate self-conscious creation of certain individual artists,"[10] such as Gilbert and Sullivan, whose cartoon rendering of Japan was never intended to fool anybody. Chesterton speaks the commonest sense in his review of *The Mikado* ("I doubt if there is a single joke in the whole play that fits the Japanese. But all the jokes in the play fit the English."[11] Its ostentatiously theatrical character relies upon and reproduces Japan's reputation as pure artifice—a reputation supported by Rudyard Kipling in his musings on Japan:

> It would pay us to establish an international suzerainty over Japan: to take away any fear of invasion and annexation, and pay the country as much as ever it chose, on condition that it simply sat still and went on making. It would *pay* us to put the whole beautiful thing. . . . the whole Empire in a glass case and mark it *Hors Concours*, Exhibit A.[12]

[10] "The Decay of Lying" (1891), in *Critical Writings*, p. 315.
[11] *The Story of the Mikado*, told by William Gilbert with intro, by G. K. Chesterton (1921).
[12] Rudyard Kipling, *From Sea to Sea* (London, 1900) vol. I, p. 455.

Japan sets the stage for a story of love that, partaking of the general character of the light opera form that Gilbert and Sullivan stirred into the modern musical, is all show. When, in *The Mikado*, the two lovers enact as mere performance the intercourse denied to them in deed by a law that prohibits all flirting, the comedy derives from the impossibility of keeping the fiction of love separate from the fact of it in the world they inhabit:

> NANKI-PO: If it were not for the law, we should now be sitting side by side, like that. [*Sits by her*]
>
> YUM-YUM: Instead of being obliged to sit half a mile off, like that. [*Crosses and sits at other side of stage*]
>
> NANKI-PO: We should be gazing into each other's eyes, like that. [*Gazing at her sentimentally*]
>
> YUM-YUM: Breathing sighs of unutterable love—like that. [*Sighing and gazing lovingly at him*]
>
> NANKI-PO: With our arms round each other's waists, like that. [*Embracing her*]
>
> YUM-YUM: Yes, if it wasn't for the law.
>
> NANKI-PO: If it wasn't for the law.
>
> YUM-YUM: As it is, of course we couldn't do anything of the kind.
>
> NANKI-PO: Not "for worlds!"[13]

The joke that Yum-Yum and Nanki-Po play here takes in more than the general ontology of the theater; it alludes to a whole nation cast as a work of art. Everything in *The Mikado*, most importantly the safe desire that propels its plot, is established by the chorus of Japanese Nobles who introduce it:

> If you want to know who we are,
> We are gentlemen of Japan;
> On many a vase and jar—
> On many a screen and fan,
> We figure in lively paint
>
> . . . .

[13] William Gilbert and Arthur Sullivan, *The Mikado* in *Complete Plays*, p. 312. All subsequent quotations of *The Mikado* refer to this edition.

49

Perhaps you suppose this throng
Can't keep it up all day long?
If that's your idea, you're wrong.[14]

The throng of artificial Japanese continues their song until the end of the play: all of its action is contained by it. Like the oriental objects that one can touch and handle, the lacquerwork and carved ivories that Dorian Gray calls a means of inculcating "the artistic temperament," the floating world of *The Mikado* supplies local habitation and a name for passions light enough to carry on stage, and agreeable enough to be left at the church door. (For all its fun, the passion performed in *The Mikado*, like the pleasures of Bunburying and the passion of the Ernestosexual, cooperates utterly with the demands of the law, here resolved into a single edict forbidding "non-connunbial affection." When love proves inconvenient for the successful resolution of the plot, which enforces this edict by rendering it unnecessary, the lover simply drops the subject).

If the aesthetic character of Japan renders it a suitable theater for the production of desire lite, the process of its aestheticization supplies a paradigm and a catalyst for its production. In his guide to Japan, Wilde remarks not merely Japan's aesthetic character, but the process of its aestheticization:

If you set a picture by Hokusai, or Hokkei, or any of the great native painters, beside a real Japanese gentleman or lady, you will see that there is not the slightest resemblance between them. The actual people who live in Japan are not unlike the general run of English people; that is to say, they are extremely commonplace, and have nothing curious or extraordinary about them. In fact, the whole of Japan is a pure invention. There is no such country, there are no such people. One of our most charming painters went recently to the Land of the Chrysanthemum in the foolish hope of seeing the Japanese. All he saw, all he had the chance of painting, were a few lanterns and some fans. He was quite unable to discover the inhabitants. . . . He did not know that the Japanese people are, as I have said, simply a mode of style, an exquisite fancy of art. And so, if you desire to see a Japanese effect, you will not behave like a tourist and go to Tokio. On the contrary, you will stay at home, and

[14] Ibid., p. 299.

steep yourself in the work of certain Japanese artists, and then, when you have absorbed the spirit of their style, and caught their imaginative manner of vision, you will go some afternoon and sit in the Park or stroll down Piccadily, and if you cannot see an absolutely Japanese effect there, you will not see it anywhere.[15]

As he proceeds in this passage from the modest claim that Japan as it is depicted in art does not actually exist outside of it, to the bolder announcement that Japan *only* exists there, Wilde records the wholesale exodus of Japan into the region of *Japanoisme*. If the misguided tourist who goes to Tokyo in the hope of discovering Japan finds the place abandoned, that is because the entire population has left town to take up residence in or on paintings, fans and tea cups, or in the style that is implied there.

As usual, Wilde's cheek is only the nerve to pronounce an ideological operation that others do not think to say out loud. Like the belief that the Japanese are great technicians, a belief that expands metonymically into the motion that the Japanese themselves *are* technology, Wilde's account, which begins by noticing the skill of Japanese artists, and ends by celebrating all of Japan as a work of art, locates the land of the rising sun as a site, more generally, for the process of aestheticization. To remark the persistence of the tendency that Wilde exhibits with his customary brazenness to locate Japan as the launching point for a flight into the realm of the aesthetic, consider its more recent proposition in the work of a critic whose eloquent aloofness from the spirit of apology rivals the temperament that a century earlier had the audacity to call the critic an artist. When Roland Barthes looks at Japan, he sees *The Empire of Signs*: "The author has never, in any sense, photographed Japan. Rather, he has done the opposite: Japan has starred him with any number of 'flashes'; or better still, Japan has afforded him a situation of writing."[16] Parting company with Wilde, Barthes's aesthetic appreciation for Japan declines the impulse to imagine that the floating world he invokes as an occasion to ponder the conditions of

---

[15] "The Decay of Lying," 315–16.

[16] Roland Barthes, *Empire of Signs*, translated by Richard Howard (New York: Farrar, Straus, and Giroux, 1982), p. 4.

language is all there is to the place. Barthes knows well the imperial episte-
mology that enables his predecessor's insouciance about the objective reali-
ties of the East: "Today there are doubtless a thousand things to learn
about the Orient: an enormous labor of *knowledge* is necessary (its delay
can only be the result of an ideological occultation)." It is all the more
telling, therefore, that "Japan" serves so brilliantly for Barthes as a landscape of signs and the conditions that enable them, that even after all is
said and done by way of ideological exposé, "Japan," at least by the light
touch of a theorist so fine, is still light enough to light up the art of the
sign and the sign of art.

　　We can catch the Japanese contribution to the aesthetization of
desire on the first page of a text famously obsessed with the subject. Here
is the opening of *The Picture of Dorian Gray*:

> The studio was filled with the rich odour of roses, and when the light summer
> wind stirred amidst the trees of the garden, there came through the open
> door the heavy scent of the lilac, or the more delicate perfume of the pink-
> flowering thorn. From the corner of the divan of Persian saddle-bags on which
> he was lying, smoking, as was his custom, innumerable cigarettes, Lord Henry
> Wotton could just catch the gleam of the honey-sweet and honey-coloured
> blossoms of a laburnum, whose tremulous branches seemed hardly able to
> bear the burden of a beauty so flame-like as theirs.[17]

The safety of the studio, filled with the luxuries of art and artifice, is compromised by its exposure to the outdoors—the heavy scent of the lilac
intrudes through the open door, but, more importantly, so does the sight
of the laburnum, caught in a tremulous embrace of a flame-like beauty,
not unlike that of a young man destined by the dictates of nature to fade.
This arboreal analogue to a passion for the novel's show-stopping hero is
displaced, as the passage continues, by figures of art:

> And now and then the fantastic shadows of birds in flight flitted across the
> long tussore-silk curtains that were stretched in front of the huge window,
> producing a kind of momentary Japanese effect, and making him think of

[17] *Dorian Gray*, p. 7.

52

those pallid jade-faced painters of Tokio who, through the medium of an art that is necessarily immobile, seek to convey the sense of swiftness and motion.[18]

Retreating from the involuntary tremblings of a compelling passion, the first thing to be seen in the safety zone arranged by the pains of the aesthetic is a "Japanese effect," a wholly fantastic figure, as removed from "the burden of a [natural] beauty so flame-like" that it would burn anyone who seeks to play with it as a "medium of art that is necessarily immobile" from "the sense of swiftness and motion." More than that though: put in mind of "those pallid jade-faced painters of Tokio" as he removes himself from the vicissitudes of the elements that his author placed outdoors, Lord Henry is put in the mind of a culture that renders the countenance of Japan as faces in jade. If the indoor landscape of the aesthetic features the familiar figures of the floating world, the journey there is guided and fueled by the impulse to artifice that defines more than Oscar Wilde's vision of Japan.

[18] Ibid.

THREE _____

OSCAR WILDE, ERVING GOFFMAN, AND
THE SOCIAL BODY BEAUTIFUL

Who wouldn't want it?

"How sad it is!" murmured Dorian Gray, with his eyes still
fixed upon his own portrait. "How sad it is! I shall grow old,
and horrible, and dreadful. But this picture will remain
always young. It will never be older than this particular day
of June. . . . If it were only the other way! If it were I who
was always young, and the picture that was to grow old!"[1]

T HE DIFFERENCE, of course, between the general yearning to look
forever young, a yearning as inescapable as the specter of fashion
that propels it, and the particular version of this desire uttered
here is that, unlike anyone else's, the dream of Dorian Gray comes true.
As "monstrous" as it is to "think," the "mad wish" he "uttered" "that he
himself might remain young, and the portrait grow old" is "fulfilled"
(78). And if the story of someone who secures the appearance of eternal youth merely by uttering the wish to do so is as fantastic as a child's
sense that, simply by wanting it, he is responsible for a change in the
weather or the death of his father, this fairy tale describes in condensed
form a spirit of voluntarism that pervades the atmosphere of Wilde's society, and societies beyond, a spirit of voluntarism that crowds our own
cosmetic counters, weight rooms, and elective surgery offices; the spirit of
voluntarism which believes that the way we look to others can be decided
by our own determinations.

   The magical thinking of *Dorian Gray* has a less miraculous, but
still impressive, analogue in the control that Wilde's characters, at least

---

[1] Oscar Wilde, *The Picture of Dorian Gray* (1891), edited by Donald L. Lawler (New
York: Norton, 1988), pp. 25–26. All subsequent citations will refer to this edition.

those who inhabit what he calls "good society," exert over their appearance, characters such as the butler in *An Ideal Husband*—"a mask with a manner"[2]—or the dandy to whom he is attached, who even under the duress of international intrigue or domestic scandal always seems to know that his buttonhole is adjusted to the best possible effect, or his feminine counterpart in society whose "affectation of manner has a delicate charm."[3] Such feats of self-presentation are familiar fixtures in Wilde's book:

> Mabel Chiltern is a perfect example of the English type of prettiness, the apple-blossom type. She has all the fragrance and freedom of a flower. There is ripple after ripple of sunlight in her hair, and the little mouth, with its parted lips, is expectant, like the mouth of a child. She has the fascinating tyranny of youth, and the astonishing courage of innocence. To sane people she is not reminiscent of any work of art. But she is really like a Tanagra statuette, and would be rather annoyed if she were told so.[4]

Mabel Chiltern and her kind are as well composed and well known as the aphorisms their author assigns to them to ventriloquize. What distinguishes the one from the other, though, is that, while we cannot help but recognize the aphorism as the work of a remote author, we cannot help but regard the character as a performance entirely self-fashioned. If Mabel Chiltern would be "rather annoyed if she were told" that "she is really like a Tanagra statuette," that is only because such a characterization would give the credit for her work to someone else. Can anyone imagine that such a type has left any aspect of her appearance to chance, especially those aspects that seem least cultivated, anyone, that is, who has read a word of Wilde, or who senses, even without reading him, simply by partaking of the culture that he helped to define, that "[b]eing natural is simply a pose?"[5] Only someone as jejune as the designated straight man in a Wilde routine would think that the least element of this well-wrought figure was

---

[2] Oscar Wilde, *An Ideal Husband*, Act 3 in *The Oxford Critical Edition of Oscar Wilde* (Oxford: Oxford University Press, 1989), p. 439. All subsequent citations of *An Ideal Husband* refer to this edition and page numbers will be cited parenthetically in the text.

[3] *An Ideal Husband*, p. 109.

[4] Ibid., pp. 110–11.

[5] *Dorian Gray*, p. 10.

unintended by her, as jejune as the observer naive enough to think that there is really anything about the dandy's mode of dressing that he has not designed, except, of course, what he has designed as such:

> His mode of dressing, and the particular styles that from time to time he affected, had their marked influence on the young exquisites of the Mayfair balls and Pall Mall club windows, who copied him in everything that he did, and tried to reproduce the accidental charm of his graceful, though to him only half-serious fopperies.[6]

Of course such fashionings of the self differ in more than degree from the alchemy that Dorian Gray accomplishes. As impressive as they are, the artful self-presentations that are the signature style of high society in Wilde's book can never hope to achieve the miracle of Dorian Gray, by which the most recalcitrant element of appearance, which even the quickest and brightest cannot hope to govern, suddenly bends to the will of its subject. Even the most resourceful presentations of the self must stop, as if for death, at the limits of the body. Thus, the most important element of this presentation in the world that Wilde describes is the one least susceptible to the agency of the self; the most vital element of this presentation is that which the self is least able to *present*. No one, apart from Dorian Gray, can will for himself the good looks that "make princes of those who have it." Such beauty is "higher than Genius. . . . It is one of the great facts of the world, like sunlight, or spring-time or the reflection in dark waters of that silver shell we call the moon. It cannot be questioned. It has its divine right of sovereignty. It makes princes of those who have it."[7] For those who know Wilde, these lines are as much a surprise as the sight of a libertine who all of sudden makes the sign of the cross. For here, the most illustrious of prophets for the priority of the cultural hails the body beautiful as a primal fact of nature before which all the powers of human contrivance fall silent. This lustrous body makes its entrance less like a figure on stage than the dawning of a heavenly light; the show-stopping incandescence of the lovely face can no more be willed by the self who is

---

[6] Ibid., p. 100.
[7] Ibid., p. 23.

WILDE, ERVING GOFFMAN, SOCIAL BODY BEAUTIFUL

blessed by it, or by one who is not, than a season or a planet can be brought into being by aesthetic fiat; the divine prerogatives of good looks can no more be acquired, even by the most cunning sense of style, than a man can crown himself king.

But if Dorian Gray's willed transfiguration is beyond the scope of mere mortals, his example nevertheless describes an avenue by which the presentation of the self is able to evade the obduracy of the body. Well before the advent of cosmetic interventions invasive enough to reshape it, Wilde suggests a means not of reforming the body but rather of replacing it with a preferred one. It would be difficult to overestimate the stakes involved in this act of surrogacy, at least by Oscar Wilde's count. As we will see, the strategy of substitution by which the self is able to undo the limits imposed by his own natural physique and exchanges a decaying, defective body for one youthful and beautiful, enables him to escape from the exterminating exclusions that Wilde's society visits on those whose appearance fails to meet the standards of physical acceptability.

We will return to assess this strategy, but first I want to notice that the sense of theatrical agency that reaches its terminus ad quem in the miracle of Dorian Gray extends well beyond the rarefied region of Wilde's society. The knack for self-presentation that Wilde attributes to his characters may appear at first glance as far removed as the steps of a ballet from our own pedestrian walks, but by the lights of a theorist most closely associated with the concept of self-presentation, such power of self-fashioning is the stuff of everyday life in the modern social world. We can take the measure of the agency that Erving Goffman grants the self to orchestrate the way he appears to others by contrasting his subject to the subject of surveillance that another social theorist has made far more famous in recent years. Compare the way Goffman describes the broad effects of the mild or traumatic surprise that routinely arises "[w]hen an individual feels he is sheltered from others' view, and suddenly discovers he is not" to the subject Foucault describes. Here is Goffman:

> At such moments of discovery the discovered individual is likely to assemble himself hurriedly, inadvertently demonstrating what he lays aside and what he puts on solely for others. In order to guard against these embarrassments,

and in order to generate within himself other persons' view of him, the individual may maintain presentability even when alone.[8]

For those schooled in the contemporary disciplines of literary and cultural studies, it is easy at first glance to confuse Goffman's subject here with that of Foucault: the subject whose good behavior is underwritten by the sense of an audience from whom he can never fully shield himself is as familiar to us as the blueprint of the panopticon—as familiar as the pressure of potential surveillance that works to enforce the intricate rules and regulations that define proper conduct in "social gatherings" a pressure of potential surveillance persuasive enough to induce its subject to toe the line even when he is home alone.

Less familiar, though, to the disciplines that have taken to heart Foucault's model of the subject who internalizes the expectations of an effectively omniscient audience is Goffman's appreciation for the power of this subject to shape what others see. The actor at home on the broad stage Goffman calls "the social world" exerts a degree of autonomous artistic control over the performance he is compelled to produce that his most accomplished theatrical counterpart would be proud to own.

To invoke one of Goffman's own key terms, the stress he places on the autonomy of "[t]he individual . . . constrained to sustain a viable image of himself in the eyes of others" may be illuminated by the frame of his study. For, however eloquent his eccentricities, however delicate and original his local insights, Goffman after all inhabits the broad context of a mid-century American sociology, concerned to define the sphere of social determination as the backdrop for the drama of individual freedom rather than the pessimistic structuralism inclined to regard the drama of individual freedom as little more than a prop in the theater of social determination.

By Goffman's lights, the demands of propriety enforced by the specter of uncontainable surveillance are less the form of the individual's oppression than the condition of his creativity, less the shades of the prison house than a theatrical script or musical score. In Goffman's admiring eyes, the conformity of this subject to the often exquisite exactions that

---

[8] Erving Goffman, *The Presentation of Self in Everyday Life* (New York: Doubleday, 1959), p. 41. All citations of *The Presentation of Self* will refer to this edition.

govern his appearance in society is matched or even eclipsed by his power to arrange it. Thus, for example, the subjection of this subject to the complex rules of engagement that govern his behavior before a real or phantom audience, rules that dictate the precise degree as well as the proper occasion for the show of "involvement," is difficult to notice next to the éclat with which he satisfies their dictates. "A [general] rule against 'having no purpose,' or being disengaged [in public] is evident in the exploitation of untaxing involvements to rationalize or mask desired lolling," Goffman observes, the "veneer of acceptable visible activity" such as "minimal 'recreational' activities" serves as "cover for disengagement, as in the case of 'fishing' off river banks where it is guaranteed that no fish will disturb one's reverie."[9] The more specific obligation to lock one's step with the "proceedings" that define what Goffman calls "focused gatherings"—church, weddings, funerals, conferences—is visible only in the dance performed to uphold the letter, while evading the spirit, of the law. "Thus, in some urban public libraries, the staff and the local bums may reach a tacit understanding that dozing is permissible as long as the dozer first draws a book and props it up in front of his head."[10]

Like the high-wire artist whose grace becomes vivid in the face of the disaster that interrupts it, the general competence of those who enact the prescribed performances of everyday life is thrown into relief when someone falls from the not-too-much–not-too-little tightrope that is the path of propriety:

> Whatever the prescribed . . . involvement[], and whatever [its] approved intensity, we usually find, at least in our middle-class society, that the individual is required to give visible evidence that he has not wholly given himself up to this main focus of attention. Some slight margin of self-command and self-possession will typically be required and exhibited. This is the case even though this obligation often must be balanced against the . . . obligation to maintain a minimum of an acceptable main involvement.
>
> Ordinarily the individual can so successfully maintain an impression of due disinvolvement that we tend to overlook this requirement. When a real crisis comes, which induces his complete absorption in a situated task, the crisis

[9] Ibid., p. 58.
[10] Ibid., p. 55.

itself, as a new social occasion, may conceal, exonerate, and even oblige what would otherwise be a situational delict. During minor crises, however, when the individual has cause to withdraw from the general orientation of the gathering but has no license to do so, we may witness wonderfully earnest attempts to demonstrate proper disinvolvement in spite of difficulties. Thus, when a man fully invests himself in running to catch a bus, or finds himself slipping on an icy pavement, he may hold his body optimistically stiff and erect, wearing a painful little smile on his face, as if to say that he is really not much involved in his scramble and has remained in situationly appropriate possession of himself.[11]

Like any failed performance, the "wonderfully earnest attempts" that Goffman reviews here by contrast illuminate the accomplishment of a successful one. The "body optimistically stiff and erect, wearing a painful little smile" falls below a standard that the subject of surveillance, charged with what Goffman calls "the presentation of self" in everyday life, is usually able to sustain; this standard of performance is refined enough to require that the act it elicits efface any sign that it is compelled at all— "Ordinarily the individual can so successfully maintain an impression of due disinvolvement that we tend to overlook this requirement."[12]

---

[11] Erving Goffman, *Behavior in Public Places: Notes on the Social Organization of Gatherings* (New York: The Free Press, 1963), p. 60. All citations *Behavior in Public Places* will refer to this edition.

[12] Whether or not this is the author's intention—and who could tell?—the word Goffman uses here ("disinvolvement") to describe a kind of comportment whose defining mark is its apparent carelessness echoes a term that Castiglione employs to describe it in his classic manual on the arts of social performance: *disinvoltura*—the genre of self-presentation whose labor is to appear unlabored.

> Therefore that may be saide to be a verie arte, that appeareth not to be arte, neither ought a man to put more diligence in any thing than in covering it: for in case it be open, it looseth credite cleane and maketh a man little set . . . Which of you is it that laugheth not when our maister Peter-paul daunceth . . . with such fine skippes, and on tipto, without moving his heade, as though hee were all of wood, so heedfully, that truly a man woulde weene hee counted his paces. What eye is so blind, that perceiveth not in this the disgrace of curiositie ["the ungracefulness of affectation"] and in many men and women here present, the grace of that not regarded agility ["that nonchalant ease"] and slight conveyance (for in the motions of the bodie many so terme it) with a kind of speaking or smyling, or gesture, betokening not [to care], and to minde any other thing more than that, to make him believe that looketh on, that he can not doe

But to the extent that the subject in Goffman's account is the master of his performance, he is determined by the social protocols that script it. To take the measure of this subjection, we need only compare the intentionality that Goffman attributes to the subject of performance with the agency that contemporary accounts ascribe to subjects who parody the social scripts that establish the identities of gender and sexuality. While taking care to complicate the concept of what she calls "theatrical agency" care to measure the limits of volition that can be attributed to the subject of such performances, Judith Butler suggests where such agency may be still be found:

> It is in terms of a norm that compels a certain "citation" in order for a viable subject to be produced that the notion of gender performativity calls to be rethought. And precisely in relation to such a compulsory citationality that the theatricality of gender is also to be explained. Theatricality need not be conflated with self-display or self-creation. Within queer politics, indeed, within the very signification that is "queer," we read a resignifying practice

---

amisse. (*The Book of The Courtier by Count Baldassare Castiglione Done into English by Sir Thomas Hoby* [1561], with an introduction by W.H.D. Rouse, and critical notes by Drayton Henderson [Everyman's Library, No. 807] [New York: E. P. Dutton, 1923], pp. 46–47.)

The air of detachment that signals the grace of the courtier (*sprezzatura*) is translated by Goffman into a more general social skill: all the social world may be a stage by his account, but the jig is up, or at least interrupted, once the actor shows the strain of knowing that he is putting on an act. Invoking *The Book of the Courtier*, deliberately or not, Goffman intimates the impressive breadth of thought about the presentation of self in society. Obviously this is not the place to canvas, much less comprehend, the history of this complex terrain, but I would, however, like to isolate one element of this history in which Goffman may be placed. The "arte, that appeareth not to be arte," the naturalist artifice that Castiglione singles out for praise in the passage quoted above reappears in contemporary efforts to describe the social causes and effects of manners, only now the presentation of the self is arranged by more or less anonymous forces rather than the actor himself. Pierre Bourdieu "*dress, bearing*, physical and verbal *manners* . . . [t]he principles em-bodied in this way are placed beyond the grasp of consciousness" (emphasis in original): that is, placed far beyond the agency of the subject who performs them. See Pierre Bourdieu, *Outline of a Theory of Practice*, translated by Richard Nice (Cambridge: Cambridge University Press, 1977) p. 94. Declining to choose between the terms of this antinomy—a self with the savoir faire to seem nonchalant, and an unknowing one; between a society that appreciates a good performance and a society that determines it—Goffman admires the accomplishments of self-presentation without bothering much to decide exactly where credit is due.

in which the desanctioning power of the name "queer" is reversed to sanction a contestation of the terms of sexual legitimacy. Paradoxically, but also with great promise, the subject who is "queered" into public discourse through homophobic interpolations of various kinds takes up or cites that very term as the discursive basis for an opposition. This kind of citation will emerge as theatrical to the extent that it mimes and renders hyperbolic the discursive convention that it also reverses. The hyperbolic gesture is crucial to the exposure of the homophobic "law" that can no longer control the terms of its own abjecting strategies.[13]

Quite unlike the transgressive agency that Butler sketches here, the intentionality that Goffman attributes to the presentation of self in everyday life is enlisted not to reject or resist society, but rather to secure its acceptance. When his subject mocks the social role he reiterates, he does so unwittingly; he does so not because, as with the counterdiscursive strategists of a new social movement whom Butler pictures in this passage, he has successfully prosecuted his intentions, but rather because he has failed to do so. Thus for example Goffman observes the ordeals undertaken by the inmates of an insane asylum to meet the demands for involvement that define proper behavior in public:

> Sometimes the patient gives the impression that he knows he cannot hope to contain himself in the situation and is now concerned merely with giving others some impression of being properly present. In Central Hospital I observed one patient who would walk from one end of the day-room to the other, where there was a doorway leading out to the porch, bravely attempting to give the impression that there was something on the porch he had to see to, and then, without entering the porch, retrace his steps and repeat the cycle. Another patient, a young psychotic woman, with the incredibly rapid tempo of a patient with motor excitement, seemed to attempt to squeeze herself back into the situation by dumping one ashtray into another, one bowl of water into another, one plate of food into another, apparently in the vain hope that it would look as though she were doing something acceptable and meaningful.[14]

---

[13] Judith Butler, *Bodies That Matter: On the Discursive Limits of "Sex"* (New York: Routledge, 1993), p. 232.

[14] Goffman, *Behavior in Public Places*, pp. 54–55.

These farcical or tragic repetitions of more ordinary presentations of the self are enacted without the glorious costumes of political purpose: the actors who perform them are queer in the old-fashioned sense of one whose earnest efforts to imitate normality have been baffled, rather than the renovated one of the rebellious hero who, by means of a hyperbolic embrace of the abnormal identity assigned to her, manages to upset the regime that dispenses such assignments.

Goffman has his own word for the awkwardness routinely covered up by the glamour that mantles contemporary rehabilitations of the queer. His word, of course, is *stigma*, the "spoiled identity" of the social loser made to bear a mark of disgrace that disqualifies her from membership in society. Some who bear this mark are able by the ingenuity of their self-presentation to pass as normal, like the mulatto, the homosexual, and the "ex–mental patient" who can sometimes "conceal information about [her] real social identity," and can thus exchange the exclusions visited on the abnormal for the fear that others "may discover that they are in the company of what in effect they demand but . . . haven't obtained,"[15] or, in the language of the melodrama that Oscar Wilde wrote and lived, the terror "every moment" "lest the mask should be stripped from one's face."[16]

Elsewhere though the stigma that disqualifies its subject from the privileges of social membership is too obtrusive to be hidden by any feat of self-presentation. First amongst the species of stigma whose recalcitrant visibility defeats the theatrical agency that would conceal it are bodily marks impossible to hide or change, marks of ethnicity, disability, or deformity that recall the etymology of the term: "The Greeks . . . originated the term *stigma* to refer to bodily signs . . . the bearer was a . . . blemished person, ritually polluted, to be avoided, especially in public places."[17]

Goffman's catalogue of spoiled identity features a range of bodily stigmas that even the most artful presentation of the self could do little to obscure. But along with the indelible marks of illness, accident, or ethnic

[15] Erving Goffman, *Stigma: Notes on the Management of Spoiled Identity* (New York: Simon & Schuster, 1963), p. 73.
[16] Oscar Wilde, *Lady Windermere's Fan*, Act 3, in *Collected Plays* (London: Methuen, 1988) p. 77.
[17] Goffman, *Stigma*, p. 3.

difference, there is another stigma, one that this catalogue omits, less drastic and thus more elusive than those that the society we inhabit, or at least inhabits us, associates with a missing or a slanted eye: that attached to any woman's face that fails to meet a standard of sexual attractiveness. Silent on this topic in his full-scale study of spoiled identity, Goffman lightly touches on it elsewhere:

> An interesting fact about the proper composition of the face is that the ease of maintaining it in our society would seem to decline with age, so that, especially in the social class groupings whose women long retain an accent on sexual attractiveness, there comes to be an increasingly long period of time after awakening that is required to get the face into shape, during which the individual in her own eyes is not "presentable."[18]

The uncomposed face of the aging woman bears a passing but profound resemblance to the disfigured one that Goffman takes up in *Stigma*: "Before her disfigurement Mrs. Dover had . . . enjoyed traveling, shopping, and visiting her many relatives. The disfigurement of her face, however, resulted in a definite alteration in her way of living . . . she seldom left her . . . home, preferring to remain in her room."[19] In both cases its deformation is radical enough to bar the blemished face not only from public acceptance, but also from public view. Their derogation extends beyond the downcast or denigrating eyes of others to include the revocation of the opportunity to be mocked or avoided by these eyes in the first place.

For Wilde, as for Goffman, the theatrical agency of the self stops at the border of the body; for Wilde, as for Goffman, the consequences of a body that fails to meet the standard of social acceptability are often grave. In Wilde, this standard is at once more broadly exacting and more exact than the one that, in Goffman's account, keeps only the aging woman at home: the demand that she fails to fulfill is a universal requirement in the world that Wilde inhabits and describes. Predicting the tendency of our own culture to put both sexes through the gauntlet of the fashion runway, designed traditionally for one only, the care his text takes to rank men's looks is no less assiduous than the trouble that others take on behalf of

---

[18] Goffman, *Behavior in Public Places*, p. 28.

[19] F. Macgregor et al., *Facial Deformities and Plastic Surgery* (Springfield, Ill.: C. Thomas, 1953), quoted in Goffman, *Stigma*, p. 12.

the female body alone. If Wilde's habit of remarking which man's face makes the grade and which does not—"You—well, of course you have an intellectual expression, and all that. But beauty, real beauty, ends where an intellectual expression begins"—is still able to startle us slightly, that is due at least as much to its deviation from the custom of exempting men from such judgments as to the homosexual imagination that this deviation brings to the surface.[20]

More widely applied in Wilde's book, the standard that defines public presentability as the "sexual attractiveness" of youth is also more strictly interpreted there. The criteria that circulates in Wilde's book specify not merely the young body, but more particularly "the slim thing, gold haired like an angel," the rose-white youth that, in Eve Kosofsky Sedgwick's words, "stood at the same time for a sexuality, a sensibility, a class, and a narrowly English national type."[21]

If in the glamorous world that Wilde helped to write, "there is absolutely nothing . . . but" the "narrowly English national type" he calls "youth," at least not for very long, that is not because those who fail to meet this mark decide to stay away. It is rather because the integrity of this charmed circle is assured by external forces, such as a habit of narrative representation that regularly excludes anyone who dwells outside it from the scene of the story. Thus, in *The Picture of Dorian Gray* nobody who falls very far from a bodily standard represented by the "young man of extraordinary personal appearance," whose portrait stands at the center of the room as the story begins and ends, lasts for very long in the novel's field of vision. Like the "rough uncomely assistant" who comes to transport the picture of Dorian Gray and then quickly disappears, those who fail to meet the specifications of beautiful youth set out by the novel are removed as quickly as possible, thus clearing the field of any sight but "the glamour of rose-white boyhood." At its most avid, this narrative tendency cancels the appearance of the unpreferred body the very moment it arrives on stage. The artist whose "rugged strong face" and "coal black hair" is no match for "the ivory and rose leaves" of his subject disappears from view

---

[20] *Dorian Gray*, p. 24.

[21] Eve Kosofsky Sedgwick, "Nationalisms and Sexualities: As Opposed to What?" in *Tendencies* (Durham: Duke University Press, 1993), p. 151.

even before he is introduced to it: "in front of [the portrait], some little distance away, was sitting the artist himself, Basil Hallward, whose sudden disappearance some years ago caused . . . such public excitement."[22] Less fantastic than the magic force that enables the hero to conceal the sight of his decomposing face while sustaining a public aspect forever young and beautiful, the policy of population control prosecuted by *The Picture of Dorian Gray* works more quietly to promote the same end.

　　Sometimes as discreet as an eye that never wanders far from a body type projected by Hollywood or the House of Windsor, the inclination to police the boundaries of a society whose visible emblem is the fair-haired youth that Wilde and his heirs never tire of celebrating elsewhere takes the form of a more violent impulse to remove all others. Consider the fate of the unlovely outsider in "Lord Arthur Savile's Crime," the fortune-teller who appears like the "sight of the Gorgon's head."[23] To the eyes of one who "had lived the delicate and luxurious life of a young man of birth and fortune, a life exquisite in . . . its beautiful boyish insouciance." The murderous fate that he reads in the hero's hand is no more horrible than his own face and fingers while he does so: "A shudder seemed to pass through him, and his great bushy eyebrows twitched convulsively, in an odd, irritating way they had. . . . Then some huge beads of perspiration broke out on his yellow forehead, like a poisonous dew, and his fat fingers grew cold and clammy."[24] Like the killer Wilde celebrates in "Pen, Pencil, and Poison"—"When a friend reproached him with the murder of Helen Abercrombie he shrugged his shoulders and said, 'Yes; it was a dreadful thing to·do, but she had very thick ankles' "[25]—Lord Arthur is driven to execute the fortune-teller as much for his "fat, flabby face," "sickly feeble smile," and "sensual mouth," as to fulfill the destiny he has predicted for him. Literalizing the underworld euphemism, killing this sorry specimen is a matter of "making him disappear":

---

[22] *Dorian Gray*, pp. 9, 50.

[23] Oscar Wilde, "Lord Arthur Savile's Crime," in *Complete Shorter Fiction*, edited by Isobel Murray (New York: Oxford University Press, 1995), p. 26. All citations of "Lord Arthur Savile's Crime" refer to this edition.

[24] Ibid., p. 24.

[25] Oscar Wilde, "Pen, Pencil and Poison," in *Complete Works of Oscar Wilde* (New York: Harper & Row, 1989), p. 1006.

In a moment he had seized Mr. Podgers by the legs, and flung him into the Thames. There was a coarse oath, a heavy splash, and all was still. Lord Arthur looked anxiously over, but could see nothing. . . . Once he thought that he caught sight of the bulky misshapen figure striking out for the staircase by the bridge, and a horrible feeling of failure came over him, but it turned out to be merely a reflection, and when the moon shone out from behind a cloud it passed away. At last he seemed to have realized the decree of destiny.[26]

Like that of another Arthur, the decree of destiny that this one fulfills extends beyond the scope of a single individual: by arranging the disappearance of "the bulky misshapen figure" of his "Nemesis," he removes his like from a world of "beautiful boyish insouciance." The mixed society in which Lord Arthur meets the palm reader at the start of the story, a "reception . . . even more crowded than usual," where "pretty women" in "their smartest dresses" mingle with "a heavy Tartar-looking lady, with tiny black eyes" and "stout prima-donna[s]," yields to an unbroken vision of a purer one at the end of the story, after "the bulky misshapen figure" has been forced out of it:

When [Lord Arthur's] wedding took place, some three weeks later, St. Peter's was crowded with a perfect mob of smart people. . . . everybody agreed that they had never seen a handsomer couple than the bride and bridegroom. . . . Some years afterwards, when two beautiful children had been born to them, Lady Windermere came down on a visit to Alton Priory, a lovely old place. . . . [She] looked wonderfully beautiful with . . . her large blue forget-me-not eyes, and her heavy coils of golden hair. Or pure they were—not that plate straw colour that nowadays usurps the gracious name of gold, but such gold as is woven into sunbeams or hidden in strange amber. . . . [She sat] with Lady Arthur . . . one of the most beautiful girls in London . . . watching the little boy and girl as they played up and down the rose-walk, like fitful sunbeams.[27]

"Passing away" like the shadow of a cloud, the thing of darkness that pollutes the atmosphere of "rose-white youth" takes his entire race with him, clearing the way for the aryan pastoral that is the story's final image:

[26] Ibid., p. 49.
[27] Oscar Wilde, "Lord Arthur Savile's Crime," pp. 50–51.

a society from which all but the most authentic blonde hair and blue eyes have sunk from view.

Wilde could hardly do more to show that protecting a "world where there is absolutely nothing but the body of blonde youth" involves methods broader than the merely personal qualms that deter anybody else from showing up there. At the same time that he amplifies the objective force of the protocol that determines public presentability, however, he also extends the capacity of those subjected to this force to satisfy its requirements. A subject whose physical features fail to satisfy the ruthless demands of what, with little risk of hyperbole, we might call a regime of body-fascism can still qualify as a member by substituting for his own physical aspect a surrogate one, like the picture of Dorian Gray, or, closer to home, the rhetorical figures fashioned by Lord Henry, whose own face, with its "olive complexion" and lines of age, while "interesting," is hardly the ticket for admission to the high society of the body beautiful which is the only one that counts in his book: "youth is the one thing worth having." With only the genius of his speech to declare, Lord Henry enters the company of beautiful youth in an access of eloquence by which his own defective body gives way to one fully qualified to join that company without flinching:

> He played with . . . [an] idea, and grew willful; tossed it into the air and transformed it; let it escape and recaptured it; made it iridescent with fancy, and winged it with paradox. The praise of folly, as he went on, soared into a philosophy, and Philosophy herself became young, and catching the mad music of Pleasure, wearing, one might fancy, her wine-stained robe and wreath of ivy, danced like a Backhand over the hills of life, and mocked the slow Silenus for being sober. Facts fled before her like frightened forest things. Her white feet trod the huge press at which wise Omar sits, till the seething grape-juice rose round her bare limbs in waves of purple bubbles, or crawled in red foam over the vat's black, dripping, sloping sides. It was an extraordinary improvisation. He felt that the eyes of Dorian Gray were fixed on him, and the consciousness that amongst his audience there was one whose temperament he wished to fascinate, seemed to give his wit keenness, and to lend colour to his imagination. He was brilliant, fantastic, irresponsible. He charmed his listeners out of themselves, and they followed his pipe laughing.

Dorian Gray never took his gaze off him, but sat as like one under a spell, smiles chasing each other over his lips, and wonder growing grave in his darkening eyes.[28]

In an exercise of theatrical agency that Goffman's "heroes of dissimulation" might well envy, whose facility for passing allows them, against all sorts of odds, to "mix with the crowd," Lord Henry joins the ranks of the body beautiful, exchanging the "worn expression" of his face for the fresh figures of his rhetoric. The spellbinding power of his speech manages not only to transform Folly, Philosophy, and Pleasure into bodies as "fleet, joyous," and youthful as the picture of Dorian Gray, it manages as well to make him one with those bodies. It's not just that he praises the soaring figure of folly, he merges with it: "The praise of folly, as *he* went on, soared into a philosophy, and Philosophy herself became young" (emphasis added). By the power of his speech, Lord Henry not only incarnates Philosophy, he makes that body his own: who is it but he who makes facts flee like frightened forest things? What is the enchanting thing from which Dorian Gray cannot withdraw his gaze but the renovated aspect of Lord Henry himself, not the olive-coloured face and worn expression, but rather the ravishing figure of "Philosophy herself [become] young," whose "white feet trod the huge press . . . till the seething grape-juice rose round her bare limbs in waves of purple bubbles"?

More than most aspects of self-presentation, "linguistic messages are felt to be voluntary and intended," Goffman remarks.[29] They are surely more so, at least by Wilde's lights, than the "wrinkled, worn and yellow face" and "coal-black hair" that mark the denigrated physique not only with the signs of age, but also with unpreferred designations of class and race. "Linguistic messages," are surely more "voluntary and intended" in Wilde's book than the body of the author occulted by it, whose shape and tone, unlike those of his words—"My Irish accent was one of the many things I forgot at Oxford"[30]—could hardly be purged of an ethnic element intolerable in a society of "rose-white youth."

---

[28] *Dorian Gray*, pp. 37–38.
[29] Goffman, *Behavior in Public Places*, p. 14.
[30] Richard Ellmann, *Oscar Wilde* (New York: Randon House, 1988), p. 38.

By means of this new figure, Oscar Wilde, and others besides, conspire to soar above a limit no less steep than that of the body itself, a limit that describes not only the difference between life and death, health and illness, but also between those who make the social scene and those who are regularly exterminated from it. Such presentations of the self, by no means everyday, may be seen to join the metaphysical achievement of theatrical agency celebrated by queer theory as a triumph over the rule of the social. Shows as artful as Lord Henry's performance or the transvestite masquerades that celebrate sexual difference even in the act of suspending it are at least as committed to gaining admittance to a society whose rules they evade as to upsetting its premises: far more so in the case of the labor that Wilde and his kind undertake to be beautiful: a labor that seeks to fashion a body as glamorous as the one they desire, which social forces as great as any count the only one fit to be seen.

FOUR

THE IMPORTANCE OF BEING BORED:
THE DIVIDENDS OF ENNUI IN
THE PICTURE OF DORIAN GRAY

My story is much too sad to be told,
But practically ev'rything leaves me totally cold
—Cole Porter, "I Get a Kick out of You," *Anything Goes*

ELIEVE IT OR NOT, there is still a secret left to be told about *The Picture of Dorian Gray*, a secret no less open, only less sensational, than the scandalous passions all but named in the novel that all but exposed the secret of its author's own. Let's face it, the book is boring: for all the thrill of *Dorian Gray*, long stretches of the story are almost unbearably uninteresting. If the fanfare of illicit excitement generated in the novel and by the novel has mostly managed to keep this secret unspoken, it has scarcely succeeded in keeping it unfelt.[1] If the engrossing rumor of covert desires attached to *Dorian Gray* distracts us for a while from our boredom with the novel, it is finally no more to be denied than the more pressing urges that everyone knows nothing can stop.

Such lapses of interest in the novel reflect lapses of interest in the novel: the ennui it induces mirrors the ennui it describes; the tedium of the reader mimics the tedium that prevails in the "poisonous book" she reads. One difference, though, distinguishes the boredom of *Dorian Gray*'s readers from the boredom of its characters: as often as ours goes without saying, theirs is a matter deemed worthy of remark. If boredom

---

[1] One exception is W. H. Auden: "Of his non-dramatic prose, we can still read *The Happy Prince and Other Tales* with great pleasure, and *The Soul of Man Under Socialism* and *Intentions*, for all their affectation, contain valuable criticism, but 'The Portrait of Mr. W. H.' is shy-making and *The Picture of Dorian Gray* a bore"; W. H. Auden, "An Improbable Life," in *Forewords and Afterwords*, edited by Edward Mendelson (New York: Vintage, 1973), p. 322.

with the novel is rarely inclined to speak its name, the boredom within it never loses its voice. What another expert in ennui calls too sad to be told is a chronic complaint in *The Picture of Dorian Gray*. Too languid to compete for the novel's center stage with more exciting events, more vehement emotions, the sideline murmurs of boredom are nonetheless never out of earshot: "It is such a bore putting on one's dress clothes";[2] "the letters . . . bored him"; "He bores me dreadfully, almost as much as he bores her"; "[T]he only way a woman can ever reform a man is by boring him so completely that he loses all possible interest in life"; "My friends were bored. I was bored"; "They have become . . . tedious"; "It is so tedious a subject"; "I had been in the room about ten minutes . . . talking to tedious academicians"; "The generation into which I was born is tedious"; "Her guests this evening were rather tedious"; "Yes it was certainly a tedious party."[3]

Listening to these voices, we may well wonder how anyone so absorbed by ennui has the energy to mention it with such élan, wonder how anyone who suffers so is capable of stifling a yawn long enough to say it so well. For surely, if only slightly, such exertions of expression contradict the state they describe: behind the elegant aspect of knowingness that boredom wears in, and beyond, *The Picture of Dorian Gray*, the prosaic condition of bodily fatigue lurks like a lingering disease. Dandies like Oscar Wilde may have fashioned sophistication's signature style out of the cloth of ennui, but they did nothing to sever its attachment to the drabbest material of daily life, nothing to separate the been-there–done-that *fatigue* of the blasé attitude from the basic grey matter of being tired.

Boredom's garrulous attaches may briefly defy, but they hardly defeat, the state they represent. Their little feats of eloquence may levitate for a moment above the condition which gives them rise, but they are helpless to annul it. Not even boredom's most captivating testimony can win its release from the enervated body to which it is fastened; not even the most charming circumlocutions can alter, though they may obscure, the physical conditions that define the terms of its labor in *The Picture of*

---

[2] Oscar Wilde, *The Picture of Dorian Gray* (1891), edited by Donald Lawler (New York: Norton, 1988), p. 28. All subsequent citations of *The Picture of Dorian Gray* refer to this edition.

[3] Ibid., pp. 11, 18, 39, 69, 79, 80, 126, 136, 140.

Dorian Gray. Even when he is suited in ennui's most elegant attire, the bored subject is still little more than a weary body at the end of the day: "There has not been a scandal in the neighbourhood since the time of Queen Elizabeth, and consequently they all fall asleep after dinner" (136).

Not quite asleep, but apparently on the verge of it, the prostrate body of Lord Henry Wotton sprawled on the first page of the novel is the first admission of the world-weariness that clings to everything in *The Picture of Dorian Gray*, like the smoke of his "innumerable cigarettes." Manifested in his recumbent posture before it is heralded by his verbal acrobatics, the boredom the dandy remarks upon with his usual wit and wisdom is embodied as well in his "tired looks" and "tired eyes"; the ennui he announces in lucid phrases can be heard as clearly in the listless voice that speaks them—"he answered listlessly"; "he [spoke] languidly"; the boredom sketched by the scandalous aphorism is signaled as well by the feeble gesture of the exhausted body—"he opened [his letters] list-lessly"; "[he] . . . rose up wearily."

And even where the body that suffers such pains of exhaustion is nowhere to be seen, it is never far from the subject of ennui; no matter how remote, the enervated physique remains the model that defines the burden of boredom in *The Picture of Dorian Gray*, where all complaints about it rely on the diagnostic vocabulary of bodily fatigue: "Like all people who try to exhaust a subject, he exhausted his listeners"; "I am tired of rose leaves"; "I am tired of myself tonight."[4]

While boredom itself can't, let us now take leave of the body for a moment to observe another aspect of this condition in *The Picture of Dorian Gray*: its intimate relation with the more glamorous condition to which it is opposed in the novel, the state of desire. The contrast between desire's affluence and boredom's poverty of affect couldn't be more apparent: Where desire possesses, or better, is possessed by, all the thrill of investment, boredom is known by its lack, characterized by the condition of indifference catalogued in *The Picture of Dorian Gray*: "He looked . . . indifferent"; "you are indifferent to everyone"; "Don't be so indifferent";

[4] Ibid., pp. 35, 116.

"Lord Henry shrugged his shoulders"; "Dorian shrugged his shoulders"; "Don't shrug your shoulders like that"; "My dear fellow, as if I cared."[5]

As different as day and night, desire and boredom are also as close, and not only in *The Picture of Dorian Gray*. A psychoanalyst designates boredom as a period of waiting for desire, or, more exactly, a period during which the psyche fends off, and thus also manifests, the unbearable (because double) burden of desiring desire. Adam Phillips: "We can think of boredom as a defense against waiting, which is, at one remove, an acknowledgment of the possibility of desire."[6] More straightforward and more familiar than the one that the psychoanalyst postulates, boredom's relation to desire in *Dorian Gray* is no less uncomfortable for that. The end of desire, rather than its prelude, the symptom and effect of desire's cessation, rather than the ambiguous prediction of its advent, the ennui that pervades *The Picture of Dorian Gray* is the dull hangover that comes after "nights of . . . misshapen joy," the listless state of "sitting alone, in the morning-room, looking very much bored" that follows the nocturnal thrills of desire:

> There are few of us who have not sometimes wakened before dawn . . . after . . . one of those nights of . . . misshapen joy. . . . Out of the unreal shadows of the night comes back the real life that we had known. We have to resume it where we had left off, and there steals over us a terrible sense of the necessity for the continuance of energy in the same wearisome round of stereotyped habits.[7]

Like its counterpart, the state of desire is also framed by a body in *The Picture of Dorian Gray*, but one as different from the other as two bodies can be. Barely noticeable in any case, boredom's unremarkable physique is even harder to see in the novel next to the one suffused with all the vivid tones of passion. So faint that some labor of discovery is often required to detect it as one at all, the body of boredom is further crowded from view by one whose dramatic definitions loom too large to leave any room for doubt: "When our eyes met, I felt that I was growing pale. . . .

[5] Ibid., pp. 13, 41, 116, 118, 140, 145.
[6] Adam Phillips, "On Being Bored," in *On Kissing, Tickling and Being Bored: Psychoanalytic Essays on the Unexamined Life* (Cambridge: Harvard University Press, 1993), p. 76.
[7] *Dorian Gray*, pp. 98, 102.

I knew that I had come face to face with someone fascinating"; " 'How I worship her!' . . . Hectic spots of red burned on his cheeks. He was terribly excited"; "You . . . have had passions . . . whose mere memory might stain your cheek with shame."[8]

And who has eyes left to observe boredom's feeble athletics—nothing more than a shrug of the shoulders, an indifferent look, the dull suffering of fatigue—when the vivid calisthenics performed by the body of desire are on display in the same gymnasium: "The lad started and drew back. . . . There was a look of fear in his eyes, such as people have when they are suddenly awakened. . . . His finely-chiseled nostrils quivered, and some hidden nerve shook the scarlet of his lips and left them trembling"; "We kissed each other. . . . She trembled and shook like a white narcissus."[9]

While in Wilde's novel the pale physique of ennui appears to have as little in common with the one ravished by desire as the one spotted in the gym or on the street has to do with the one that never is, they are actually the same body seen in different lights. As surely as night turns into day, the vibrant body of desire turns into its listless counterpart. The desiring subject slips into the state of ennui in *The Picture of Dorian Gray*, and in Wilde's corpus more generally, as often as exhaustion hits the body where it dwells: "The fantastic character of these instruments fascinated him, yet, after some time, he wearied of them";[10] "Perhaps," the narrator in "The Portrait of Mr. W. H." surmises, "by finding perfect expression for a passion, I had exhausted the passion itself. Emotional forces, like the forces of physical life, have their positive limitations."[11] According to the diagnosis that Wilde prefers everywhere, and never more so than in the novel where he dreamed of its unfettering, desire declines for the simple reason that the body to which it is attached, either by means of a discreet metaphor or a frank comparison, can't keep it up.[12]

---

[8] Ibid., pp. 11, 20, 47.

[9] Ibid., pp. 21, 62.

[10] Ibid., p. 105.

[11] Oscar Wilde, "The Portrait of Mr. W. H.," in *The Artist as Critic: Critical Writings of Oscar Wilde*, edited by Richard Ellmann (Chicago: University of Chicago, 1982), p. 212–13.

[12] Wilde's announcement that all passion is spent sounds a little like the scenarios of its systematic cessation that emerged in social theory of the late nineteenth century—the "blasé

Thus the bodily fatigue that frames the experience of boredom for Wilde also designates its ultimate cause: if being bored is a matter of being tired, getting bored is a matter of getting tired. Of course, other, more prominent suspects have a hand in the death of desire chronicled again and again in Wilde's story; better-known genealogies of boredom are duly rehearsed by the novel: the spots of commonness revealed when the loved one removes her stage makeup; the callowness of a lover whose desire cannot endure the sight of them; and, most familiar of all, the satisfaction of desire that is also its end. But even in the absence of these conditions, the dissolution of desire is assured by the limits of the body that almost always defines it in *The Picture of Dorian Gray*. As unremarkable as the need for sleep, the bodily exhaustion that underwrites desire's decline in *Dorian Gray* is also as unmentionable as the dread of death. If the subject of ennui is cast there as a weary body, it is also cast as a dying one:

> The pulse of joy that beats in us at twenty becomes sluggish. Our limbs fail, our senses rot. We . . . [are] haunted by the memory of the passions of which we were too much afraid, and the exquisite temptations that we had not the courage to yield to.[13]

---

attitude" that Georg Simmel diagnosed as the symptom of a money economy, the disenchantment that Max Weber called the hallmark of modernity, and the pale shallowness that their Frankfurt School heirs took as the one dimension of a subjectivity held captive by capitalism. But Wilde's rendering of passion's disappearance has less in common with such historical explanations than it does with the picture of desire's bodily limits sketched by a founder of political economy. Here is Christopher Herbert's summary of what he calls the "problem of desire" in Malthus, the problem with which several generations of political economists were preoccupied:

> Malthus['s] . . . image of mankind in its original state goes a long way to qualify the received notion of the human organism as driven by irresistible and innate "bodily cravings." For he insists strongly that man in the primitive state is driven by scarcely any cravings at all beyond a monotonous need for food. . . . On the contrary, the main human traits in the (hypothetical) state, and the ones which Malthus evidently regards as the permanent ones of the human biological constitution, are sluggishness, listlessness, amorphousness, inertia. . . . The problem of desire in Malthus is not, as in Hobbes, that it is too powerful and unruly. . . . Rather it is that man in his natural condition is so *feeble*. (Christopher Herbert, *Culture and Anomie: Ethnographic Imagination in the Nineteenth Century* (Chicago: University of Chicago Press, 1991), pp. 112–13).

[13] *Dorian Gray*, pp. 23–24.

Here the cessation of desire, where all that is left is "the *memory* of the passions of which we were too much afraid," the *memory* of "exquisite temptations that we had not the courage to yield to" is a strain of boredom from which no one recovers, rather than the one that a good night's sleep will cure. While such full frontal views of the body bored to death are as rare as those that Dorian Gray allows of the picture he keeps secreted in an attic room, it is nonetheless a regular, if subliminal, figure in Wilde's novel: "When a man says that [he has exhausted life], one knows that life has exhausted him"; "he was sick with that terrible ennui, that terrible tedium vitae."[14]

And even when the exhaustion of boredom stops short of the one that predicts the body's final rest, it is still a source of sorrow in *The Picture of Dorian Gray.* Insinuated amongst the sounds that herald the arrival of the morning "after one of those nights of . . . misshapen joy" are the sounds of mourning, "the sigh and sob of the wind. . . . wandering round the silent house."[15] Less lethal than a sickness unto death, but grievous nonetheless, the fatigue that arises as routinely as the sun in and beyond *The Picture of Dorian Gray* is the boredom that Adam Phillips thoughtfully calls "the mourning of everyday life."[16]

The grim weariness that underwrites the recession of desire in Wilde's novel casts in the gravest light the glib comfort with which his dandy greets it: "The only difference between a caprice and a life-long passion is that a caprice lasts a little longer;" "The worst of having a romance of any kind is that it leaves one so unromantic." The ease that allows the dandy to fashion epigrams out of the sentence of bodily exhaustion appears at first glance to confirm the quality of stoicism that Baudelaire famously conferred upon him, a stoicism no less heroic, but rather more so, for its air of insouciance, a stoicism that exerts itself in an apprehension, unflinching for all its listlessness, of the awful truths that others take nervous pains to mask under the opiate of optimism.

---

[14] Ibid., pp. 113, 138.
[15] Ibid., pp. 101–2.
[16] Adam Phillips, "On Being Bored," p. 71.

But the dandy's submission to the hard fact of desire's decline is too eager to fully pass itself off as the decorous "deference to reality" that Freud called mourning's final achievement. Like the secret longing for a long-anticipated death, the dandy harbors a never quite covert desire for desire's termination. However much his constitution inclines toward indolence, Lord Henry, as if contracted to conduct a campaign of saturation advertising, could hardly be more industrious finding new opportunities to mention passion's tendency to recede. The delight the dandy takes in his slogans—"Lord Henry struck a light on a dainty silver case, and began to smoke with a self-conscious and satisfied air, as if he had summed up the world in a phrase"—extends beyond a love of his own form to embrace as well the event that it publicizes.

Not to say that this love of boredom is often open-handed: unlike the man who, trapped in women's clothes, proceeds to make a spectacle of himself by enjoying his sentence too visibly, the *amor fati* hidden within the worldly knowledge that no love lasts seldom blows its cover. The embrace of ennui is usually camouflaged by a sophistication whose languid fingers lift only to hail its destined arrival; the desire for desire to be done is concealed by the cynicism that calls it brief by nature; the impulse to prescribe the limits of passion is hard to tell from the impulse merely to describe them—"You should not say the greatest romance of your life. You should say the first romance of your life." "[T]he people who love only once in their lives are really the shallow people. What they call their loyalty, and their fidelity, I call either the lethargy of custom or their lack of imagination. Faithfulness is to the emotional life what consistency is to the life of the intellect—simply a confession of failure."[17]

The dandy's hankering for desire to end gains further cover from the scandal provoked in the novel by the announcement that it has: "I hate the way you talk about your married life, Harry. . . . I believe that you are really a very good husband, but that you are thoroughly ashamed of your own virtues"; "You don't mean a single word of all that, Harry; you know you don't"; " 'Stop!' faltered Dorian Gray, 'stop! you bewilder me.' "[18] The hue and cry that arises when the end of desire is proclaimed,

[17] *Dorian Gray*, p. 43.
[18] Ibid., pp. 10, 20, 61.

a clamor of outrage and anxiety as predictable as a reaction to a dinner bell, or the straight man's response to the funny one's shtick, obscures the interests of those who proclaim it. Manifestly unwanted by those who hear of it, the speaker's own desire for the recession he announces is therefore allowed to pass unnoticed.

But like the nervous tic that surfaces on even the most studied mask of insouciance, the dandy's impatience for the play of passion to close can't be kept altogether out of view by any pose of fatalism or device of distraction. Always implicit in the pleasure he takes in telling it, the dandy's investment in desire's recession sometimes emerges altogether from the closet of necessity where it is usually concealed. Being "a good deal bored with each other" he admits in "The Decay of Lying," "is one of the objects of the club." And in *Dorian Gray*, the dandy candidly wishes that his protégé's passions will be brief—"I hope that Dorian Gray will make this girl his wife, passionately adore her for six months, and then suddenly become fascinated by someone else"—while frankly grieving not the death of passion, but rather its too persistent life: "I once wore nothing but violets all through one season, as a form of artistic mourning for a romance that would not die."[19]

· · · · ·

The perverse preference that Wilde's dandy expresses, sometimes implicitly, sometimes right out loud, for the state of boredom where desire ceases over the state of desire itself may seem like business as usual in the world of a writer for whom the reversal of received hierarchies is a matter of rhetorical habit and doctrinal conviction. Such a denigration of desire appears more anomalous, though, when it is placed next to the gospel of passion upon which his author staked his life. For if the dandy Wilde fashioned welcomes, with varying degrees of explicitness, the death of desire, Wilde himself, as everyone knows, was practically killed defending it:

> The "Love that dare not speak its name" in this century is such a great affection of an elder for a younger man as there was between David and Jonathan, such as Plato made the very basis of his philosophy. . . . It is in this

[19] Ibid., pp. 61, 80.

century misunderstood, so much misunderstood that it may be described as the "Love that dare not speak its name," and on account of it I am placed where I am now. It is beautiful, it is fine, it is the noblest form of affection. There is nothing unnatural about it. . . . it repeatedly exists between an elder and a younger man, when the elder man has intellect, and the younger man has all the joy, hope and glamour of life before him. That it should be so the world does not understand. The world mocks at it and sometimes puts one in the pillory for it.[20]

The discordance between the dandy's distaste for the state of desire and his author's defense of it becomes sharper still when we hear the dandy himself testify on passion's behalf. Like Wilde on the stand, abandoning his wisecracks and languor long enough to speak for passion in a passionate voice, Lord Henry, dropping his own, rises to the heights of Paterian enthusiasm as he calls his protégé to the vocation of desire:

People are afraid of themselves, nowadays. . . . The terror of society, which is the basis of morals, the terror of God, which is the secret of religion, these are the two things that govern us. . . . And yet . . . I believe that if one man were to live out his life fully and completely, were to give form to every feeling, expression to every thought, reality to every dream—I believe that the world would gain such a fresh impulse of joy that we would forget all the maladies of mediaevalism, and return to the Hellenic ideal—to something finer, richer, than the Hellenic ideal, it may be. But the bravest man amongst us is afraid of himself. Every impulse that we seek to strangle broods in the mind, and poisons us.[21]

But while the eloquence of Lord Henry's advocacy matches Wilde's own, they are separated by more than the difference between the pages of a novel and the docket at Old Bailey. For if, like Wilde, Lord Henry is wholehearted in his praise of passion, unlike Wilde he is quite indifferent when it comes to praising specific ones. Sounding more like an industry-wide advertisement for a whole category of commodity than a promotion for a particular brand, more like the aesthete who urged the "study and worship" of "all beautiful things" than the defendant compelled to explain his

[20] This is Wilde's famous speech at his first trial, in response to cross-examination; quoted by Richard Ellman in *Oscar Wilde* (New York: Vintage Books, 1988), p. 463.
[21] *Dorian Gray*, p. 20.

love for one kind of beautiful thing, Lord Henry endorses *every* feeling, thought, dream, and impulse, rather than any in particular.

To be sure, the impulses and temptations Lord Henry shelters under the general rubric of desire bear the tell-tale marks of a specific strain of it, the one discouraged by the twin terrors of God and society whose full flowering would signal the renaissance of Hellenism, and for which Wilde himself was hounded all the way to the grave. But its usefulness as a strategy of euphemism hardly comprehends the dandy's allegiance to the broad category of desire, or his corresponding lack of interest in its particular forms.

If the big tent of Desire is unfolded in *The Picture of Dorian Gray* as a cover under which the love that dare not speak its name is allowed to remain unspoken, a resort to the safety of the generic as familiar as the abbreviation of friend for boyfriend, it is extended there for the benefit of quite different loves as well:

> Dorian Gray falls in love with a beautiful girl who acts Juliet, and proposes to marry her. Why not? . . . Every experience is of value, and whatever one may say against marriage it is certainly an experience. I hope that Dorian Gray will make this girl his wife, passionately adore her for six months, and then suddenly become fascinated by someone else.[22]

Assimilating it to the general "experience" of fascination, Lord Henry is reconciled to a marriage disadvantageous both to Dorian Gray, and, what is more remarkable, to himself. His devotion to the category of desire is catholic enough to overcome even the self-love that is the most enduring staple of his personality. Despite his own desire for it, Lord Henry greets the news of Dorian Gray's preference for an actress without "the slightest pang of annoyance or jealousy."[23] Any slight that Lord Henry might suffer when the boy he desires desires someone else instead is a narcissistic wound too small to heed in the face of the subtler pleasure that comes from observing the boy desire anything at all:

> Lord Henry watched him with a subtle sense of pleasure. How different he was now from the shy, frightened boy he had met in Basil Hallward's studio!

[22] Ibid., p. 61.
[23] Ibid., p. 48.

His nature had developed like a flower, had borne blossoms of scarlet flame. Out of its secret hiding-place had crept his Soul, and Desire had come to meet it on the way.[24]

Lord Henry's commitment to the generic cause of Desire takes form specifically in the nonpartisan campaign he conducts throughout the novel to multiply its general population. Taking a page from Pater, and anticipating the rules of a game show whose contestants race down the aisles of a supermarket in a rush to accumulate as many items as they can during an allotted interval, Wilde's dandy impresses his student with the task of "getting as many [passions] as possible into the given time"—"[B]e always searching for new sensations."

The proliferation of passions for which he campaigns is enabled rather than contravened by the cessation of individual passions, which Lord Henry welcomes, since according to a rationing scheme that prevails in *The Picture of Dorian Gray*—and, beyond that, in an inclination to serial monogamy whose force has only been confirmed in the years since the compulsions, both institutional and intimate, to monogamy per se have flagged—each subject is allotted only one passion at a time, and therefore one must pass away to make room for another.

As ubiquitous as it is familiar, the rule of one desire at a time is assumed both by the denunciation of adultery heard in *Lady Windermere's Fan*—"you who have loved me . . . have . . . pass[ed] from the love that is given to the love that is bought"[25]—as well as by the desire for it we have already heard manifested in *The Picture of Dorian Gray*. However much they differ in their interpretation of it, both the lady and the libertine abide by a law of restricted desire that various administrations have done nothing to relax: both the outraged moralism of the first and the outrageous immorality of the second take for granted that loving one person requires leaving another.

Reaching past the homosexual, and the heterosexual as well, the desires whose proliferation Lord Henry advocates are not confined to those featured in the domestic melodrama or erotic adventure story. The

[24] Ibid., p. 47.
[25] Oscar Wilde, *Lady Windermere's Fan*, Act 1, in *The Complete Plays* (London: Methuen, 1989), p. 47.

passions that crowd the life of his protégé include not only the intrigues with women that the novel mentions, and the entanglements with men that it almost does, but also "mad hungers" for other items on a shopping list as long and miscellaneous as the book itself: the exquisite actress he adores and the brooding scientist he loves without saying so share billing on an agenda of desire whose other objects include "Sevres china" and "a chased silver Louis-Quinze toilet-set"; a "gilt Spanish leather [screen], stamped and wrought with a rather florid Louis-Quatorze pattern"; statuettes and a "little table of perfumed wood thickly incrusted with nacre"; fine art and fancy food; oriental narcotics and "Persian rugs"; "embroideries" and "textiles"; "jewels" and "Venetian glass."[26]

Extending beyond both sanctioned and scandalous species of sexual passion, the desires that Lord Henry encourages include as well the up-market varieties of consumer demand. In an essay that suggestively sketches relations between the Aestheticism of *The Picture of Dorian Gray*, concentrated in Lord Henry's anthem for desire, and the theories and practices of late-nineteenth-century capitalism, Rachel Bowlby detects various alliances and analogies between the novel's promotion of beauty, fashion, and pleasure, and the promotions designed by the contemporaneous discourse of advertising. She remarks, for example, that Dorian Gray resembles a "walking advertisement" for eternal youth and beauty, and that there was a "growing habit during this period of commissioning famous artists to design advertisements."[27] But Bowlby's apprehension of an "implicit convergence of the ideals of advertising and aesthetics" stops short of remarking their actual identification in *The Picture of Dorian Gray*.[28] The intimacy between advertising and aesthetics sometimes surpasses the practice of reciprocal borrowing that Bowlby documents, where two independent campaigns enlist each other's themes and services. Lord Henry's promotion of desire is not merely "like an advertisement," it *is* an advertisement, albeit for every commodity, rather than any commodity in particular. The universal desire he seeks to inculcate is less a homology for consumer demand than a totality that comprehends it.

[26] *Dorian Gray*, pp. 74–76, 85, 96, 105, 107, 109.
[27] Rachel Bowlby, "Promoting Dorian Gray," in *Shopping with Freud* (London: Routledge, 1993), p. 13.
[28] Ibid.

Moreover, the contribution that the call to passion sounded by Lord Henry makes to late-nineteenth-century market capitalism is more than a matter of promoting a taste for fancy goods. The general proliferation of desire that he encourages functions more broadly to support the increasingly specialized market for commodities that evolved in the second half of the nineteenth century, where, in Georg Simmel's words, "the seller must always seek to call forth new and differentiated needs."[29] The ephemerality of individual desires heralded in *Dorian Gray* can thus be read as the subjective correlative of the obsolescence built into the objects that the dandy prefers above all others, such as the cigarettes that he never stops smoking, items whose "chief charm" is that they "don't last."

•　•　•　•　•

The profits that derive from the demise of desire are not limited to the service it renders a capitalist economy. Its benefits are not restricted to facilitating an increase of the general population of desire, an increase that in turn supplies a diversifying market with the corresponding diversification of consumer demand that it requires. Beyond the satisfactions it affords the aesthete and the advertiser, the ephemerality of desire that Lord Henry promotes offers the additional advantage of relieving its subject from the horror that befalls the subject whose desire persists. To approach this horror ourselves, we turn now to consider the one form of passion that does succeed in evading the hegemony of ennui in *The Picture of Dorian Gray*.

Despite his claim to the contrary, repeated often enough and with sufficient eagerness to look like the defensive denial that Freud called negation—"The only difference between a caprice and a life-long passion is that a caprice lasts a little longer"; "The worst of having a romance of any kind is that it leaves one so unromantic"—one species of passion does manage to slip through the safety net that stops all others in *The Picture of Dorian Gray*. Not the love of men for women, or women for men, but rather the one that dares not speak its name. In a reversal of fortunes like the one at the center of the novel's plot, *The Picture of Dorian Gray* inverts

---

[29] Georg Simmel, "The Metropolis and Mental Life," in *The Sociology of Georg Simmel*, translated, edited, and with an Introduction by Kurt H. Wolff (New York: The Free Press, 1950), p. 420.

the usual organization of affections arranged by Victorian narratives, and repeated by others beyond, an organization that assigns homosexual desire the status of transitory state or transitional stage, while instating its heterosexual counterpart as passion's permanent form—"Nowadays all the married men live like bachelors and all the bachelors live like married men." In a novel that helped transform the Victorian bachelor into the suspected homosexual, Lord Henry's remark comes close to announcing the inversion of desires that is the order of the day in Wilde's story. Here promiscuity is the franchise of the husband and the straight man on the prowl—"the one charm of marriage is that it makes a life of deception absolutely necessary for both parties"; " 'Dear Lady Narborough,' murmured Dorian, smiling, 'I have not been in love for a whole week—not, in fact, since Madame de Ferrol left town.' "[30]

And here a species of homosexual passion to which the usual developmental itinerary of desire affords no place, which Wilde in court called the "great affection of an elder for a younger man," and which he depicts in *Dorian Gray* as the artist's love for the boy that he paints, is a denomination of "worship," a type of "idolatry," a form of "romance" with no end in sight. Surpassing the training grounds of the oedipal drama and the schoolyard crush—preliminary versions of homosexual desire that pass away as so much prehistory after preparing for the heterosexual romances that follow from them—the affection of an elder for a younger man is rather a love built to last: "The love that he bore him—for it was really love—had nothing in it that was not noble or intellectual. It was not that mere physical admiration of beauty that is borne of the senses, and that dies when the senses tire. It was such love as Michael Angelo had known, and Montaigne, and Winckelmann, and Shakespeare himself."[31]

If Basil Hallward's passion for Dorian Gray transcends the early stage where homosexual desire is typically confined in the culture of the Victorian novel, and in the culture that follows from it, such love also eludes the physical frame that limits desire more generally in *The Picture of Dorian Gray*. Detached from the body, the love that dares not speak its name is instead a spirit whose infinite vitality, age, and, no less remarkably,

[30] *Dorian Gray*, p. 10.
[31] Ibid., p. 93.

weariness, cannot wither. The capacity of "such love as Michael Angelo had known, and Montaigne, and Winckelmann, and Shakespeare himself" to evade the temporal limits that define the boundary of an individual life is no more miraculous than its capacity to evade the everyday fatigue that defines the boundary of an individual passion. Since it is "not that mere physical admiration of beauty that is borne of the senses, and that dies when the senses tire," "such love as Shakespeare himself" felt is equipped to transcend not only the kingdom of death, but also the rule of ennui: "As long as I live . . . Dorian Gray will dominate me," the artist declares. "You can't feel what I [Henry] feel. You change too often."[32]

The metaphysical achievement of the love that dare not speak its name is the end of a story that we all know, a tale of sublimation that begins with a shameful or illegal "impulse" that "broods in the mind" because it is denied the franchise of physical expression. In a makeover routine that has furnished the consolation of canonization for, perhaps first amongst others, generations of homosexuals, the "impulse" that "broods in the mind" is transformed into the triumph of the spirit; the desire that, at least in a widely available novel, dares not assume bodily shape is congratulated as the one that transcends bodily exhaustion.

But the familiar contract by which the pains of sublimation are rewarded with the palm of eternal form—a contract whose propagandists include Walter Pater, Allen Bloom, and Wilde himself—has a catch in Wilde's novel. While the Shakespearian desire pictured there, through the offices of sublimation, evades the limits of the body and thus achieves a durability denied physical passion in Wilde's novel, the youthful body that is the object of this desire is left behind. In "The Portrait of Mr. W. H.," the young man that the older one desires is translated, along with the desire itself, into the timeless aesthetic monument:

> His true tomb, as Shakespeare saw, was the poet's verse, his true monument the permanence of the drama. So had it been with others whose beauty had given a new creative impulse to their age. The ivory body of the Bithynian slave rots in the green ooze of the Nile, and on the yellow hills of the Cermaei-cus is strewn the dust of the young Athenian; but Antinous lives in sculpture, and Charmides in philosophy.[33]

[32] Ibid., p. 16.
[33] Oscar Wilde, "The Portrait of Mr. W. H.," pp. 208–9.

But in *The Picture of Dorian Gray*, the boy whose beauty gives a new cre-
ative impulse to his age has no such luck: the artist is unable to stretch
the labors of sublimation to include him in the sublime sanctuary they
fashion. Basil Hallward's impulse to enshrine the body he paints amongst
the durable monuments of "verse," "drama," "sculpture," and "philosophy" by confiding it to the abstract "suggestion" of a "new manner,"
found "in the curves of certain lines" and "in the loveliness and subtleties
of certain colours," can't withstand the temptation to get near the breath-
ing form that remains the real object of his desire:

> I worshipped you. . . . I grew more and more absorbed in you. . . . One day,
> a fatal day I sometimes think, I determined to paint a wonderful portrait of
> you as you actually are, not in the costume of dead ages, but in your own
> dress and in your own time. . . . as I worked at it, every flake and film of colour
> seemed to me to reveal my secret. I grew afraid that others would know of
> my idolatry.[34]

Barred from the House of Art, the body of youth in *The Picture
of Dorian Gray* is thus subject to the fate of all flesh: "Yes, there would
be a day when his face would be wrinkled and wizen, his eyes dim and
colourless, the grace of his figure broken and deformed. . . . He would
become dreadful, hideous, and uncouth." Even the famous exception to
the rule of physical decay in Wilde's story only succeeds in suspending it
temporarily: at the end of the novel and the end of his life, the apparently
ageless body of Dorian Gray is "withered, wrinkled and loathsome of
visage" having merged again with the decaying physique that haunts
it all along.

Lord Henry, whose "strange panegyric on youth" first sounds the
"terrible warning of its brevity" is as distressed by the impending ruin of
the beautiful body as he is eager to promote the proliferation of passions.
His enthusiasm for the multiplication of desires is matched by his disgust
for the decay that will destroy the gorgeous physique: "We never get back
our youth. . . . Our limbs fail, our senses rot. We degenerate into hideous
puppets"; "you have a wonderfully beautiful face, Mr Gray. . . . But . . .
[w]hen your youth goes, your beauty will go with it"; "Every month . . .

---

[34] *Dorian Gray*, p. 90.

brings you nearer something dreadful. Time is jealous of you, and wars against your lilies and your roses. You will become sallow, and hollow-cheeked, and dull-eyed"; "Someday . . . you [will be] old and wrinkled and ugly"; "Thought [will] sear your forehead with its lines, and passion brand your lips with its hideous fires."[35]

The subject who persists in desiring a physique given over to such decay is vulnerable to a voltage of disgust that emanates from the ultimately horrible body he never leaves off desiring. "Every day. I couldn't be happy if I didn't see him everyday. He is absolutely necessary to me," Basil Hallward confesses, and one day, or rather one night, his enduring interest in Dorian Gray leads him to an access of revulsion from which he never recovers. Driven by his love for the boy to see the secret of his soul, the artist is compelled to confront the ruin of his body:

> An exclamation of horror broke from the painter's lips as he saw in the dim light the hideous face on the canvas grinning at him. There was something in its expression that filled him with disgust and loathing. Good heavens! It was Dorian Gray's own face he was looking at! The horror, whatever it was, had not entirely spoiled that marvelous beauty. There was still some gold in the thinning hair and some scarlet on the sensual mouth. . . . He turned to Dorian Gray with the eyes of a sick man.[36]

No such sickness troubles the subject whose passions tire: however fatigued he may be, he is exempted, at least, from the more acute disease to which the subject of Shakespearian desire is susceptible in *The Picture of Dorian Gray.* Abandoning the adored body before it has time to grow old, the subject whose passions weary is able to keep his eyes trained on a "world" where "there is absolutely nothing but youth,"[37] a world where the ill-making spectacle of physical decay has no chance to appear.

There is evidence in the text to suggest that the senophobic excess that marks the novel's rendering of what age does to the beloved body of youth represents the displaced effects of the violence done to the homosexual in part by means of, but surely beyond, *The Picture of Dorian Gray.*

---

[35] Ibid., pp. 22–25.
[36] Ibid., p. 121.
[37] Ibid., p. 24.

If the aging body of the man that another loves is hateful in the novel, it is made so by surgical procedures filled with hate: a breaking of its form, a twisting of its limbs, a branding of its lips that surpasses anything done to the physique by the natural effects of age and weather, or even by the allegorical symptoms of his own sin. It could be that the abuse suffered by the picture of Dorian Gray is a form of corporal punishment meted out for the "strange idolatry," and the call to Hellenism that inspired the picture in the first place.

But whatever the etiology of the image that generates it, the horror in store for a man who loves another for too long in *The Picture of Dorian Gray* doubles the profits that derive from the defalcation of desire. If the rule of ennui readies its subject for ever-new labors of commodity consumption, it also allows him to avoid the sight of the spoiled body, even as it requires that he submit his own to the depredations of boredom. And as much as the anxiety to avert this sight reinforces the regime of ephemeral passion where it *can* be averted, the fortunes of market capitalism owe a debt of gratitude to the fear induced by the spectacle of physical decay, a spectacle that Oscar Wilde, and others besides, picture first of all as the ruined body of homosexual desire.

FIVE

THE PROTESTANT ETHIC AND THE SPIRIT OF ANOREXIA: THE CASE OF OSCAR WILDE

OR ALL HIS lawlessness, there is at least one venue where the subject of desire featured in *The Picture of Dorian Gray* has proven himself the most exemplary of citizens. At least by the lights of a contemporary sensibility concerned to expose what passes for natural proclivities as cultural constructions invented and imposed by the discourses that claim only to reveal them, the reprobate hero of Wilde's novel could hardly be more cooperative. As if pressed into the service of this sensibility *avant le lettre*, the story the novel tells of Dorian Gray's developing desire describes a trajectory of de-essentialism, in which his erotic passions appear less and less an expression of inherent attribute, and more and more a function of external influence; less and less like a natural hunger that arises from within the subject, and more and more like an infection or an affectation picked up by the subject who is constituted in the very act of absorbing what is alien to him—a trajectory of de-essentialism celebrated by Lord Henry, its principle prograganadist in the novel, as the conversion of "appetite into art."[1]

As the history of his sexuality begins, Dorian Gray's desires appear as the dormant urges of his nature, awakened by a famous speech that will sound, even to those who haven't read it already, like a line that they have heard before:

> There is no such thing as a good influence . . . to influence a person is to give him one's own soul. He does not think his natural thoughts, or burn with his natural passions. . . . To realize one's nature perfectly—that is what each of us is here for. People. . . . have forgotten the highest of all duties, the duty

---

[1] *The Picture of Dorian Gray* in *The Major Works*, edited with an Introduction and Notes by Isobel Murray (Oxford: Oxford University Press, 1989), p. 194. All subsequent citations of *Dorian Gray* refer to this edition.

90

that one owes to one's own self. They feed the hungry and clothe the beggar, but their own souls starve. . . . Every impulse that we strive to strangle broods in the mind, and poisons us. . . . The only way to get rid of a temptation is to yield to it. Resist it, and your soul grows sick with longing.[2]

And those who have read Wilde's novel, as well as those who have not, will well know the drama of revelation that comes next:

> "Stop!" faltered Dorian Gray, "stop! you bewilder me. I don't know what to say. . . . Let me think. Or rather let me try not to think."
>
> He was dimly conscious that entirely fresh influences were at work within him. Yet they seemed to have come really from himself. The . . . words . . . had touched some secret chord that had never been touched before, but that he felt was now vibrating and throbbing to curious pulses.[3]

Almost as soon as the speech praising them is done, though, the "natural passions" of Dorian Gray's "own soul," which Lord Henry's eloquence apparently brings out in this passage, give way to the desires of another, and this displacement of "natural passions" by alien ones only grows more blatant as the chronicle of his erotic development continues. "[T]he ideology of . . . essence implicit in Lord Henry's speech . . . produces the very 'nature' or self that it seems only to reveal,"[4] Lee Edelman remarks, and whatever quibbles might attach themselves to his concise deconstruction of the repression hypothesis Lord Henry rehearses in the novel's primal scene are quite overwhelmed by the general direction of Dorian Gray's erotic development. If the scene of sexual instruction in *Dorian Gray* is somewhat more ambiguous than Edelman's brisk poststructuralist reading of it admits, he is surely faithful to the movement of the story as a whole. Any passion or proclivity that might have dwelt within Dorian Gray before Lord Henry gets to him, any desire that might have been exposed and activated, rather than wholly produced, by his manipulations, has almost entirely disappeared by the time they are recollected the morning after:

> How charming he had been . . . the night before. . . . Talking to him was like playing upon an exquisite violin. He answered to every touch and thrill of the

[2] *Dorian Gray,* pp. 61–62.
[3] Ibid., p. 62.
[4] Lee Edelman, *Homographesis* (New York: Routledge, 1994), p. 17.

bow. . . . There was something terribly enthralling in the exercise of influence. No other activity was like it. To project one's soul into some gracious form . . . to convey one's own temperament into another as though it were a subtle fluid or a strange perfume: there was real joy in that.[5]

And that's just the beginning. From this moment on, the prospect of an essential self and a strain of desire that is the currency of that self recedes further and further from view, displaced by an apparently inexhaustible catalogue of alien ones that Dorian Gray absorbs instead, a catalogue whose first entry is a "poisonous book," "a psychological study of a certain young Parisian, who spent his life trying to realize in the nineteenth century all the passions . . . that belonged to every century except his own."

This rejection of essentialism is almost as famous an aspect of Wilde as the one that has arrested the attention of his friends and enemies since his command performance at the Old Bailey. No less well known by now is the alliance between these things proposed or assumed by a range of recent criticism, the alliance located in, and then beyond, Oscar Wilde, between perversity and postmodernism, sexual dissidence and the denial of depth, an alliance whose most fundamental link is the by-now common sense that the concept of essence is the prop of a heterosexual normativity whose propagations rely on the claim that nature is on its side.[6]

The school of queer theory that congratulates for its political subversiveness the habit of displacing the essential or natural by the interpolated or performed subject of desire, and that has found an inaugural genius in Wilde's life and work,[7] has been much criticized lately, not least of

---

[5] *Dorian Gray*, pp. 74–75.

[6] See Judith Butler, *Gender Trouble: Feminism and the Subversion of Identity* (New York: Routledge, 1990), for an inaugural situation of de-essentializing apprehension as an instrument of resistance to heterosexual hegemony.

[7] For elaborations of Wilde's status as avatar of a queer theory, which identifies the announcement and apprehension of deessentialism as an instrument of resistance to heterosexual hegemony, see Christopher Craft, "Alias Bunbury: Desire and Termination in *The Importance of Being Earnest*," in *Representations* 31 (Summer 1990): 19–46; and Jonathan Dollimore, *Sexual Dissidence: Augustine to Wilde, Freud to Foucault* (Oxford: Oxford University Press, 1991). For a skeptical account of this affiliation, see Eve Kosofsky Sedgwick, "Tales of the Avunculate: Queer Tutelage in *The Importance of Being Earnest*" in *Tendencies* (Durham: Duke University Press, 1993): 52–72, "each of these readings traces and affirms the gay possibility in Wilde's writing by identifying it—feature by feature, as if from a Most

all by the theorist whose own work has been enlisted as the core curriculum of that school.[8] It is not my intention to enter directly into this controversy. I will be concerned here not to assess the liberatory efficacy of the impulse to de-essentialize, but rather to consider the social character of this impulse along lines removed altogether from the binary topography of subversion and containment. I will read Wilde to trace a genealogy of this impulse, which suggests that, whatever its contemporary social effects, the theory and practice of de-essentialism is itself sometimes the effect of a social force situated far from the field of sexual politics, where its dimensions have typically been taken in recent years, and quite foreign to the intimate affects that charge that field, but whose invisible hand, like the distant financial cataclysm whose reverberations shake the domestic economy, helps to define their terms.

I have in mind here a social force that takes form in the specter briefly arising in *The Picture of Dorian Gray* to describe the fate of those who, evading what the libertine calls "the highest of duties," fail to appease their natural desires: "their souls starve." I will argue here that the swerve from essentialism in Wilde is as much a defense against this specter as it is resistance to the ideological conditions of heterosexual hegemony. I will argue that this specter arises in the first place to punish a proclivity associated not with the party of sexual perversity, but rather with the leisure class; a taste not for unorthodox erotic passions and practices, but rather for the abstention from labor that constitutes the canon of that class; a tendency at odds not with any protocol of sexual propriety, but rather with the compulsion to work best known as the Protestant ethic.

• • • • •

The resistance to work that usually goes without saying, a proclivity generally as understated as it is generally understood, is more blatantly exhibited in Wilde's colorful excursion into the regions of the dismal science. As

---

Wanted poster—with the perfect fulfillment of a modernist or post-modern project of meaning-destablization and identity-destabilization."

[8] Judith Butler, *Bodies That Matter: On the Discursive Limits of "Sex"* (New York: Routledge, 1993). See especially chapter 8.

removed, at least at first glance, from the charged terrain of sexual dissidence as "a more than usually lengthy lecture by the University Extension Scheme on the Influence of a Permanent Income on Thought" that nobody dreams of attending in *The Importance of Being Earnest*, the spirit of nonconformity that animates the expanded version of that lecture Wilde called "The Soul of Man under Socialism" (1891) is no less audacious than the one that landed him in Reading Gaol:

> Every man must be quite free to choose his own work. No form of compulsion
> must be exercised over him. If there is, his work will not be good for him,
> not good in itself, and will not be good for others. And by work I simply
> mean activity of any kind. . . . It is mentally and morally injurious to man to
> do anything in which he does not find pleasure, and many forms of labour
> are quite pleasureless activities and should be regarded as such.[9]

Like any utopian drive, Wilde's aspiration to end work as we know it, an aspiration sufficiently ambitious to oppose a rule of civilization hard to tell from a principle of reality, begins with conditions close to home. As things stand now, a happy few already have the high life where work is play, a site of liberty and a source of joy; a happy few dwell already in the House Beautiful where work takes its form from the disinterested delight of art; a happy few already inhabit the holiday pastoral where labor, changed utterly, cleansed of the element of compulsion to which it is typically yoked, has blossomed into pleasure; a happy few "who have private means of their own," and are thus "under no necessity to work for their living"; a happy few are "able to choose the sphere of activity that is really congenial to them and gives them pleasure."[10]

But "*every* man must be quite free to choose his own work," and as things stand now

> there are a great many people who, having no private property of their
> own, and being always on the brink of sheer starvation, are compelled to do
> the work of beasts of burden, to do work that is quite uncongenial to them,

---

[9] Oscar Wilde, "The Soul of Man under Socialism," in *The Works of Oscar Wilde* (London: Blitz Editions, 1990), p. 1021. All subsequent citations of the essay refer to this edition.
[10] Ibid., p. 1019.

and to which they are forced by the peremptory, unreasonable, degrading Tyranny of Want.[11]

By "converting private property into public wealth" and thus "ensur[ing] the material well-being of each member of the community," "Socialism, Communism, or whatever one chooses to call it" will dismantle the Tyranny of Want, and thus allow everyone, and not just the subsidized elite to do as they please; will abolish the slavery of forced labor that Marx, in a waggish inversion that Wilde himself might well have savored, called "free"; will liberate the working class from the obligation to toil for the food it needs to live and allow those who belong to it to take their rightful place in the kingdom of leisure. And so, with a stroke of a pen like a wave of a wand, Wilde envisions total victory for a principle as dear to his heart as anything: "Pleasure! What else should bring one anywhere?"[12] "What else is there to live for?"[13]

But if Wilde's socialist inclinations are in their own way as bold as a love that declines to heed a battery of discouragements as variously broad and deep as the culture that it occupies, they are even less frequently expressed. Aside from sporadic sightings here and there, Wilde's card-carrying involvement with the tradition of utopian prophecy is as brief as the length of a single essay. It may be that the yearning for a society where the tyranny of want, and thus the obligation to work, has been abolished seldom expresses itself in Wilde's book, not, as with another yearning rarely disposed to speak its name, from a lack of nerve, but rather a lack of need; not because it is scandalous, but rather because it appears superfluous.

For in the society that Wilde was pleased to know, the tyranny of want is as good as gone. The compulsion to labor could hardly be further removed from the society of conspicuous leisure that is the only one to show up on Wilde's map; the brilliant society that usually eclipses any broader one, and not only in Oscar Wilde's eyes. How could the requirement to work for a living have a hold over "anyone who's anyone" on the

---

[11] Ibid.

[12] *The Importance of Being Earnest* in *The Major Works*, p. 481. All subsequent citations of this play refer to this edition.

[13] *An Ideal Husband*, in *The Major Works*, p. 401. All subsequent citations of this play refer to this edition.

stage where his spotlight is trained—the lounging exquisite, the sardonic dowager, the well-healed misanthrope, the headstrong heiress—all those who saunter through the luxurious premises charted by a collection of writings that might just as well be called "a more than usually lengthy lecture on the Influence of a Permanent Income on Thought"?

What could the working stiff have to do with the society swell whose only occupation is a way of life defined by the "conspicuous abstention from labor"[14] which its preeminent taxonomer identified as the signature style of what he called the "leisure class"? Perhaps a little more than either might have imagined: For, as the dandy's defender knows, the labor of ostentatiously abstaining from it is no life for the slacker:

> Idle. . . . How can you say such a thing? Why, he rides in the Row at ten o'clock in the morning, goes to the Opera three times a week, changes his clothes at least five times a day, and dines out every night of the season. You don't call that leading an idle life, do you?[15]

Nice work if you can get it, but high society is no utopia, even in miniature: as routinized as the work-week from which they distinguish themselves, its rituals of leisure hardly satisfy the condition of absolute freedom that is Wilde's standard for the good life; they hardly count as "the activity" detached from "compulsion of any kind, "the activity," "congenial," "pleasurable," and "quite freely chosen" that is the only sort that Wilde's brand of socialism allows. Released from the requirement to work, the leisure-class subject is assigned instead the task of refraining from it, and if the task proves to be one, if not chosen, at least not minded by the subject to whom it is allotted, this is no more than the lucky coincidence of temperament and necessity that occurs to anyone not wholly done in by the job he has to do in any case: "It is awfully hard work doing nothing. However, I don't mind hard work where there is no definite object of any kind."[16]

No slouch himself, Wilde, when he wasn't spending it with reckless abandon, was busy throughout most of his life working for his living:

---

[14] Thorstein Veblen, *The Theory of the Leisure Class* (1899, 1912), introduction by C. Wright Mills (New York: New American Library, 1953), p. 43.

[15] *An Ideal Husband*, p. 393.

[16] *Earnest*, p. 498.

it may be, to take a page from the fairy tales, that his dedication to the protocol of the leisure class resembles the self-abnegating devotion of a misshapen troll for a haughty queen.[17] But whatever the sources of his fervor, the "conspicuous abstention from labor" is never more so than in Wilde's social register, even considering the wealth of gilded-age displays that surround it. If the pattern dandy in *An Ideal Husband* is "the idlest man in London," it must have been a hard contest to call, since the boulevards, houses, and clubs are crowded with others whose unemployment is no less assiduously underscored in Wilde's writings. The concentrated pageantry of the dandy's daily rounds is sublimated and disseminated in the care with which Wilde generally asserts the indolence of the characters he features. Like the social arbiter whose eagerness he derides—"She treats her guests exactly as an auctioneer treats his goods"—Wilde wastes no time indicating their abstention from labor, announcing it either in so many words or by habits and dispositions that may as well be: "He had set himself to the serious study of the great aristocratic art of doing nothing"; he was "a delightful, ineffectual young man with a perfect profile and no profession"; "pleasure, pleasure! What else should bring one anywhere?;" " 'Well, Harry . . . what brings you out so early? I thought you dandies never got up till twelve, and were not visible till five.' "[18]

However well documented Wilde's carelessness about other, more pressing prohibitions, no one is more respectful of the "tabu" as cardinal for high society as that against incest for society in general, and which, by Veblen's account, "comes to be . . . not only an honorific or meritorious act, but a . . . requisite of decency."[19] As much as he allows intimations of other transgressions to gather around his reprobate hero, Wilde is careful to certify his conformity to this rule of decency; as much as we are encouraged to suspect him of other vices, we are compelled to recognize his rectitude when it comes to this "index of reputability." Indeed our suspicion of the first is the implicit certification of the second, since the late-night intrigues that absorb him could only involve one who, like his counterpart or alias in the pornographic adventure, never has to

---

[17] "The Birthday of the Infanta," in *Oscar Wilde: Complete Shorter Fiction*, edited with an Introduction by Isobel Murray (New York: Oxford University Press, 1980), pp. 185–202.

[18] *Dorian Gray*, pp. 71–72; "The Model Millionaire" in *Complete Shorter Fiction*, p. 88.

[19] Veblen, *Theory of the Leisure Class*, p. 43.

worry about getting to work in the morning; and since leisure is the implicit condition for the trivial, and even less reputable, pursuits announced and insinuated in *The Picture of Dorian Gray*, those amateur interests and serious addictions that can only be a way of life for someone who never has to worry about getting to work at all.

Less acute than the tyranny that compels labor, the pressure to abstain from it, as elusive, typically, as an ambiguous admonition—"In my day, one never met anyone in society who worked for their living. It was not considered the thing"[20]—has all the force of gravity in the social world that Wilde charts; intangible, but by no means immaterial, the pang that enforces the rule of leisure is as effective in its own way as the one that enforces its counterpart. Apparently lighter than the tyranny that compels labor, the pressure to abstain from it is never too light to pass unfelt by the subject of Wilde's preferred society, no matter how immune to social pressure he is generally. The "rough-mannered old bachelor . . . whom the outside world called selfish because it derived no particular benefit from him, but who was considered generous by Society," is as indifferent to the judgment of the first as he is sensitive to that of the second. Deaf to the disapproval of the outside world, the misanthrope who "set[s] himself to the serious study of the great aristocratic art of doing nothing" could hardly be more alert to the appearance of what high society counts as the essence of impropriety:

> [He] . . . paid some attention to the management of his collieries in the Midland counties, excusing himself for this taint of industry on the ground that the one advantage of having coal was that it enabled a gentleman to afford the decency of burning a wood on his own hearth.[21]

A joke, of course, but like fire in a theater, or firearms at the airport, the "taint of industry" is a grave enough charge in Wilde's leisure-class canon that even its most facetious assertion calls for immediate investigation. If the aristocrat in question can't be serious, or only half-so about the "taint of industry" attached to his slight attention to the management of his coal mines, a taint itself tainted by the coal miners to which it is slightly

---

[20] *A Woman of No Importance*, in *The Collected Plays* (London: Methuen, 1988), p. 304.
[21] *Dorian Gray*, p. 71.

connected, he still takes the trouble to mention and dispel it. If no one else apart from the defendant himself hears the accusation of this taint, that is because it is delivered by what Simmel calls the "voice of conscience:" "The voice of conscience we hear only in ourselves, although in comparison with all subjective egoism, we hear it with a force and decisiveness which apparently can stem only from a tribunal outside the individual."[22] Mildly mocking the overwrought supervision that he nonetheless effectively embraces, the aristocrat in question, like an ironic but ultimately friendly witness before the committee on subversion, seeks to clear his name of the suspicions attached to it by the remotest of associations. His fleeting identification with the working class is terminated when, at the conclusion of his testimony, the aristocrat recalls his affiliation with the class that doesn't, when he "excus[es] himself for this taint of industry on the ground that the one advantage of having coal was that it enabled a *gentleman* to afford the decency of burning a wood on his own hearth."

But more is at stake in avoiding work than the profits of invidious comparison that Veblen's descendent calls symbolic capital.[23] If the urge to abstain from labor is an elementary form of the drive for distinction that Veblen and his followers locate at the center of society,[24] it is also the means of evading the corrosive grip of work as we know it, a regime of industry that touches all parts of the everyday hell that Wilde, in "The Critic as Artist," calls "action":

> There is no mode of action . . . that we do not share with the lower animals. . . . Action, indeed, is always easy, and when presented to us in its most aggravated, because most continuous form, which I take to be that of real industry, becomes simply the refuge of people who have nothing whatsoever

[22] Georg Simmel, "Superordination and Subordination," in *The Sociology of Georg Simmel*, translated, edited, and with an Introduction by Kurt H. Wolff (New York: The Free Press, 1950), p. 254.

[23] Pierre Bourdieu, *Outline of a Theory of Practice*, translated by Richard Nice (Cambridge: Cambridge University Press, 1977); *Language and Symbolic Power*, translated by Gino Raymond and Matthew Adamson, edited and with an Introduction by John B. Thompson (Cambridge: Harvard University Press, 1991).

[24] See Pierre Bourdieu, *Distinction: A Social Critique of the Judgment of Taste*, translated by Richard Nice (Cambridge: Harvard University Press, 1984).

to do. . . . It is to do nothing that the elect exist. Action is limited and relative. Unlimited and absolute is the vision of him who sits at ease and watches. . . . Thought is degraded by its constant association with practice. . . . Each of the professions means a prejudice. The necessity for a career forces every one to take sides. We live in the age of the overworked, and the undereducated; the age in which people are so industrious that they become absolutely stupid.[25]

A specter haunts this vision of action: labor. More than mere instances of that specter is the being we share "with the lower animals," its aspects constitute the essence of this abject sphere. Action in its "most aggravated" "form" is "real industry;" if thought is corrupted in general by "its constant association with practice," it is compromised in particular by overwork—"We live in the age of the overworked, and the undereducated"—and negated utterly by industriousness: "people are so industrious that they become absolutely stupid."[26]

As familiar as the pangs of hunger, the hardness of labor with which action in general is here identified has the feel of an inflexible sentence, like the speed of light or the Fall of Man. But no less than the pleasures of sexuality, the pains of labor can be read as social symptoms; no less than the pulsations of the erotic, the dull or acute strains of working for a living may be read as political promulgations masked as mere

---

[25] "The Critic as Artist," in *The Artist as Critic: Critical Writings of Oscar Wilde*, edited by Richard Ellmann (Chicago: University of Chicago Press, 1969), pp. 256, 275, 278. My reading of "The Critic as Artist" emphasizes one element of its historical situation. For an account of other elements of this situation, taking up some of the sexual and professional pressures that form a crucial part of the essay's social context, see Lawrence Danson's *Wilde's Intentions: The Artist in his Criticism*, chapter 6 (Oxford: Clarendon Press, 1997).

[26] Hannah Arendt situates this reduction of action in general to labor in particular at the center of a degraded modernity:

[W]e live in a society of laborers . . . we have almost succeeded in leveling all human activities to the common denominator of securing the necessities of life and providing for their abundance. Whatever we do, we are supposed to do for the sake of "making a living"; such is the verdict of society, and the number of people, especially in the professions who might challenge it, has decreased rapidly. . . . The same trend to level down all serious activities to the status of making a living is manifest in present-day labor theories.

For Arendt, this leveling down is a dark chapter in the history of ideas, which by her concentrated lights, is another name for History itself. Hannah Arendt, *The Human Condidtion* (Chicago: University of Chicago Press, 1958), p. 126–27.

facts of life. No less than sexuality, what Marcuse calls "the fundamental fact" of "more or less painful arrangements and undertakings for the procurement of the means for satisfying needs," is shaped by social contingencies that make a permanent fixture of the human condition as much the artifact of the epoch it inhabits.[27]

The tradition of critical thought most notably concerned with the social specificity of work has concerned itself in particular to take the dimensions of a historical regime of labor close to home, a historical regime that defines work as we know it, a regime we can glimpse in the figure of "real industry" that Wilde denigrates and more extensively in another phase of his quarrel with action in "The Critic as Artist:"

> Don't talk about action. It is a blind thing dependent on external influences, and moved by an impulse of whose nature it is unconscious. It is a thing incomplete in its essence, because limited by accident, and ignorant of its direction, being always at variance with its aim. . . . the man of action . . . knows neither the origin of his deeds nor their results. From the field in which he thought that he had sown thorns, we have gathered our vintage, and the fig-tree that he planted for our pleasure is as barren as the thistle, and more

[27] Herbert Marcuse, *Eros and Civilization: A Philosophical Inquiry into Freud* (Boston: Beacon Press, 1966), p. 35. Readers of Marcuse may recognize the debt the present essay owes to his work. I am indebted especially to Marcuse for a habit of connecting the social forms of sexuality with those of labor, and thus for a way of connecting the intimacies of the erotic with the macropolitics of the economic. My differences from Marcuse will also be evident: while Marcuse relies on an essentialist model of sexuality consistent with the repression hypothesis, I am concerned with a version of the erotic in Wilde consistent with the de-essentialist, constructivist perspective of Foucault in particular and postmodernism in general. Most importantly, while Marcuse casts sexuality as the target of the capitalist regime of labor, the target of a surplus repression that extends and deepens that regime, my reading of Wilde seeks to notice how the sexuality featured in his book furnishes its subject some relief from that regime. For a quite different, quite fine account of the relation between Marcuse and Wilde, see Carolyn Lesjak, "Utopia, Use, and the Everyday: Oscar Wilde and a New Economy of Pleasure," *ELH* 67 (2000): 179–204. For a canny recent revival of the alliance politics proposed by Marcuse, which reads one form of transgressive sexuality as a characteristically indirect expression of a utopian impulse to resist a work ethic that extends itself into the realm of "responsible relationships," see Laura Kipnis, "Adultery," in *Critical Inquiry* 24, no. 2 (Winter 1998): 289–327. Not the least persuasive, not to say eloquent, aspect of Kipnis's article is its insistent recognition that the utopian intensities of the transgression she treats can hardly escape an idiom as banal as the familial ideologies it seeks to evade.

bitter. . . . Each little thing that we do passes into the great machine of life which may grind our virtues to powder and make them worthless, or transform our sins into elements of a new civilization.[28]

Like the abstract art that sublimates a concrete passion, or the diffuse despair that camouflages a local pain, this panoramic picture of the *vita activa* bears signs of a more particular historical circumstance, located in the specific figure that Wilde employs here to comprehend human action, the figure of the factory where individual acts melt into the impersonal process of labor: "Each little thing that we do passes into the great machine of life which may grind our virtues to powder and make them worthless, or transform our sins into elements of a new civilization." The amputation of agency that is the casualty of action generally in Wilde's account describes in particular the condition of capitalism that Marx called alienated labor:

> The worker is related to the *product of his labour* as to an *alien* object. . . . What is embodied in the product of his labour is no longer his own. The greater this product is, therefore, the more he is diminished. The *alienation* of the worker in his product means not only that his labour becomes an object, assumes an *external* existence, but that it exists independently, *outside himself*, and alien to him, and that it stands opposed to him as an autonomous power. . . . [A]lienation appears not merely in the result but also in the process of production, within productive activity itself. . . . work is external to the worker. . . . he does not fulfill himself in his work but denies himself.[29]

> "If we follow the path taken by labour in its development from the handicraft via co-operation and manufacture to machine industry," Georg Lukacs remarks in his decisive report on the condition of alienated labor,

> we can see a continuous trend towards greater rationalization, the progressive elimination of the qualitative, human and individual attributes of the worker. . . . the process of labour is progressively broken down into abstract,

---

[28] "The Critic as Artist," pp. 256–57.
[29] Karl Marx, "Alienated Labour," in "Economic and Philosophical Manuscripts," from *Early Writings*, translated and edited by T. B. Bottomore (New York: McGraw Hill, 1963), pp. 122–27 (emphasis added).

rational, specialized operations so that the worker loses contact with the fin-
ished product and his work is reduced to the mechanical repetition of a specialized set of actions. . . . The . . . stance adopted towards a process mechanically conforming to fixed laws and enacted independently of man's
consciousness and impervious to human intervention, i.e. a perfectly closed
system, must likewise transform the basic categories of man's immediate attitude to the world. . . . Here, too, the personality can do no more than look
on helplessly while its own existence is reduced to an isolated particle and fed
into an alien system.[30]

Circulated by the broad ideological apparatus Lukacs calls "reification,"
the condition of the working class covers the entire sphere of human action in "The Critic as Artist." Here, "the . . . stance adopted towards a
process mechanically conforming to fixed laws and enacted independently
of man's consciousness and impervious to human intervention" is the de-
pressed condition of anyone who does anything; here the machine to
which Wilde, in "The Soul of Man under Socialism," remarks "man has
been . . . the slave," the machine of "real industry" where the alienation
of labor is concentrated has expanded to become "the great machine of
life which may grind our virtues to powder and make them worthless, or
transform our sins into elements of a new civilization,"[31] but which in any
case defeats even our most artful intentions.

To escape the shadow of the machine broad enough to cover all
forms of human effort, Wilde invokes a vision of absolute idleness quite
distinct from the conspicuous abstention from labor that characterizes the
condition of the leisure class. This absolute idleness echoes what Hannah
Arendt calls the "error" of an ancient idealism that condemns all action as
the annulment of the actor's agency and autonomy, and that, in her words,
locates his "salvation" "in nonacting, abstention from the whole realm of
human affairs, as the only means to safeguard one's sovereignty and integrity as a person":[32]

---

[30] Georg Lukacs, "Reification and the Consciousness of the Proletariat," in *History and
Class Consciousness: Studies in Marxist Dialectics*, translated by Rodney Livingstone (Cambridge: MIT Press, 1971), pp. 88–90.
[31] "The Soul of Man," p. 1028.
[32] Arendt, *The Human Condition*, p. 234.

Let me say to you now that to do nothing at all is the most difficult thing in the world, the most difficult and the most intellectual. To Plato, with his passion for wisdom, this was the noblest form of energy. To Aristotle, with his passion for knowledge, this was the noblest form of energy also. It was to this that the passion for holiness led the saint and the mystic of medieval days. . . . It is to do nothing that the elect exist. Action is limited and relative. Unlimited and absolute is the vision of him who sits at ease and watches. . . . The gods live thus. . . . We, too, might live like them, and set ourselves to witness with appropriate emotions the varied scenes that man and nature afford. We might make ourselves spiritual by detaching ourselves from action, and become perfect by the rejection of energy.[33]

Behind its classical sound, the cold pastoral retreat that Wilde proposes bears the traces of a distinctly modern pattern of flight. To evade the specter of labor that haunts all human activity in a world where the machine of "real industry" has become "the great machine of life," Wilde points to a region of unbroken ease, a recess illuminated now less by the wisdom of the ages than the light of the TV screen; a sphere of leisure less like the condition of classical contemplation than a day spent in bed. "[W]ith its fragmentation of labour, modern industrial civilization creates . . . a need for leisure," Henri Lefebvre observes, whose "most striking imperative"

is that it must produce a *break*. . . . Thus there is an increasing emphasis on leisure characterized as distraction: rather than bringing any new worries, obligations, or necessities, leisure should offer liberation from worry and necessity. Liberation and pleasure—such are the essential characteristics of leisure, according to the parties concerned. . . . So those involved tend to reject ambiguous forms of leisure which might resemble work or entail some kind of obligation. . . . They mistrust anything which might appear to be educational and are more concerned with those aspects of leisure which might offer *distraction*, *entertainment* and *repose*, and which might compensate for the difficulties of everyday life.[34]

[33] "The Critic as Artist," pp. 275, 277–78.
[34] Henri Lefebvre, *Critique of Everyday Life: Volume One*, translated by John Moore (New York: Verso, 1991), p. 33 (emphasis added).

What Lefebvre diagnoses here as an aversion to labor sensitive even to the slightest insinuation of its hold—the tendency "to reject ambiguous forms of leisure which might resemble work or entail some kind of obligation"— determines the idleness, that Wilde exults in "The Critic as Artist," an idleness as hollow as the holiday dedicated to "do[ing] nothing at all." For it is only when the sphere of leisure has been drawn to the point of pure passivity that it is sufficiently removed from the regime of labor, whose grasp comprehends the whole category of action.

And as if this resort to the rigorous purity of utter inanition were not enough to insure it, Wilde strives further to defend the separation of leisure and labor by propping the difference between them onto the more dramatic distance charted by an ancient opposition. Like the nineteenth-century campaign on behalf of a sexual minority that sought substantiation in classical antecedents, the platonic scheme on which it rests in "The Critic as Artist" magnifies the modern divide between work and rest, a divide which, for all its decisiveness, is often no grander than the quotidian separation of a day at work from a day off. Dressed as the difference between the ideal and the real, a distinction, elsewhere as easy to overlook as a lost weekend or a dull rerun, is radiant now in the timeless style of the Western thinker's master dichotomy. The vacuity— doing "nothing at all"—at the heart of the vacation rises to a height as far from the workplace as the serenity of philosopher and saint from the push and shove of everyday life.

The aura of ease that describes Wilde's vision of idleness here is as different, at least at first glance, as freedom and necessity from the thin atmosphere of high society where leisure is a duty that, while preferable to its counterpart, remains, nonetheless, another job to do. While the conspicuous abstention from labor that is the lifestyle of high society is marked by a pressure to conform, the leisure enjoyed by the charmed circle of the elect is marked by the ease of just looking: "Unlimited and absolute is the vision of him who sits at ease and watches." Compared to the exhibitory exertions of high society ("you don't call that idle, do you?"), this higher mode of leisure seems like a night at the movies after a day in the spotlight. " 'Ah! I have talked quite enough for today,' said Lord Henry. . . . All I want now is to look at life."[35]

---

[35] *Dorian Gray*, p. 80.

A night at the movies, but of course, by Wilde's lights, more like the antecedent forms of just looking whose collective name is the key term of his glossary. To "make ourselves spiritual by detaching ourselves from action," to aspire successfully to the condition of the elect "who sit at ease and watch," is to possess "the aesthetic temperament"; to enter the company of the gods who watch "with the calm eyes of the spectator the tragi-comedy of the world" is to join the society of the spectacle that Wilde calls the work of art, or, more precisely, the society of the spectacle that Wilde calls the detached ease of aesthetic appreciation:

> The contemplative life, the life that has for its aim not doing but being . . . that is what the critical spirit can give us. The gods live thus: either brooding over their own perfection, as Aristotle tells us, or as Epicurus fancied, watching with the calm eyes of the spectator the tragi-comedy of the world that they have made. We, too, might live like them, and set ourselves to witness with appropriate emotions the varied scenes that man and nature afford. We might make ourselves spiritual by detaching ourselves from action and become perfect by the rejection of energy. . . . Calm, and self-centred, and complete, the aesthetic critic contemplates life, and no arrow drawn at a venture can pierce between the joints of his harness.[36]

Like the contemporary advertising that promises access to the glamour of old romance by the purchase of the new commodity, Wilde promotes the aesthetic sphere as a modern facsimile of a classical ideal. Contemplating life as art, the aesthetic critic "calm, and self-centred, and complete," occupies the easy chair of a modern pantheon where "[w]e might make ourselves spiritual by detaching ourselves from action and become perfect by the rejection of energy." "[W]atching with the calm eyes of the spectator the tragi-comedy of the world," the aesthete manages to miss the bullet that never fails to reach the man of action, the arrow whose unerring aim shatters the agency of any actor, no matter how regally armored.[37]

[36] "The Critic as Artist," p. 278.
[37] Wilde alludes in this passage to 1 Kings 22:34, in which Ahab is killed in battle: "And a certain man drew a bow at a venture, and smote the king of Israel between the joints of the harness."

106

But if the fine art of leisure appears far closer to the utopia arranged for "The Soul of Man under Socialism" than the arduous regions of high society, it is no less haunted, as we might surmise even from Wilde's busy efforts to defend against it, by the form of labor whose transcendence is utopia's prehistory. For just as the rule of leisure that defines high society is enforced by a pressure softer than the threat that enforces the imperative to work (but coercive still), the ease of this higher idleness only extends by other means the passivity that prompts the flight from work in the first place. Like the committed liar who discovers much to his chagrin "that all his life he has been speaking nothing but the truth," he who rejects the Protestant ethic in order to follow "the great creed of Inaction" embraces the dissipation of agency he meant to escape; like the epigram whose insurrection against the tyranny of common sense is confined to the acrobatics of inverting it, the passive pleasure of just looking that is the main feature in Wilde's house of art is less an escape from the regime of alienated labor than a repetition of its primary aspect.[38]

In a variation on "the irony" attached to the modern ruse of power that Foucault calls the "deployment of sexuality"—"The irony of this deployment is in having us believe that our 'liberation' is in the balance"—Wilde celebrates as the "fastidious rejection" of that regime what is after all only its sublimated afterlife:[39] an extension of labor's passivity that, like a mode of subjection embraced as the means of freedom, functions to deepen its hold. Rewriting that passivity as a refined and passionate repose, the high art that Wilde celebrates renders the condition of our imprisonment an experience to be enjoyed rather than merely endured. To praise as the highest glory "the mere joy of beholding," a joy like the serenity of the gods who "watching with calm eyes passively regard" "the world that they have made" return in a spectacle of alienated majesty, is to support the "self-alienation" that, for Walter Benjamin, is the standard of modernity, a "self alienation [that] has reached such a degree that . . .

[38] *Earnest*, pp. 222, 538.

[39] Michel Foucault, *The History of Sexuality: Volume I: An Introduction*, translated by Robert Hurley (New York: Vintage Books, 1978), p. 159.

mankind . . . can experience its own destruction as an aesthetic pleasure of the first order."[40]

* * * * *

But no depth of collaboration between the idle and the rule of labor they resist can suspend the sentence imposed with the regularity of a natural law by that regime on those who do not work. As uncompromising as the most severe sexual censorship, the regime of labor is rigorous enough to mobilize itself against any exception to its rule, even those as inscribed as the weekend in the schedule of compulsory labor they appear to abjure. Even here, as we will see in a moment, the compulsion to work knows no bounds.

Were it not for the fact that no further confirmation of its wide-spanning potence could possibly surprise us, we might be more amazed that the conviction that Weber located at the heart of the Protestant ethic—that no one is ever exempt "from the unconditional command to labour"—is a law whose arm is long enough to reach the heart of its most dedicated discontents.[41] "Work is the mission of man on this Earth," Carlyle declares,[42] but such ex cathedra pronouncements have nothing over the authoritative éclat with which Wilde expounds the opposing theory of the leisure class: "There is something tragic about the enormous number of young men there are in England at the present moment who start life with perfect profiles, and end by adopting some useful profession"; "The condition for perfection is idleness";[43] "It is to do nothing that the elect exist."[44] If Wilde's book renders the injunction against labor

---

[40] Walter Benjamin, "The Work of Art in the Age of Mechanical Reproduction," *Illuminations*, edited and with an Introduction by Hannah Arendt, translated by Harry Zohn (New York: Schocken Books, 1969), p. 242.

[41] Max Weber, *The Protestant Ethic and the Spirit of Capitalism*, translated by Talcott Parsons (Los Angeles: Roxbury Publishing Company, 1995), p. 159. Subsequent citations of this work refer to this edition. On the weight of the Irish Famine on Wilde's mind, see Owen Dudley Edwards, "Impressions of an Irish Sphinx," in *Wilde The Irishman*, edited by Jerusha McCormack (New Haven: Yale University Press, 1998), pp. 47–70; Davis Coakley, *Oscar Wilde: The Importance of Being Irish* (Dublin: Town House, 1995), pp. 10, 19, 21, 109.

[42] Thomas Carlyle, *Chartism* in *Critical and Miscellaneous Essays* (London: Chapman and Hall, 1896–1899), p. 133.

[43] "Phrases and Philosophies for the Use of the Young," in *The Major Works*, p. 573. All citations of this text refer to the Oxford edition.

[44] "The Critic as Artist," p. 275.

as compelling for the "elect"—those who aspire to the condition of "perfection," or who, by virtue of their good looks, manifest their arrival there, as the commandment to perform it is for the working class, this is partly because his sense of this injunction is borrowed from the prescriptive character it opposes. Resisting authority by mirroring it, mimicking the judicial confidence attached to the law whose spirit it inverts, the trademark *attitude* that Wilde displays when he peremptorily reverses conventional verdicts would seem, by virtue of its reflective relation to them, immune to the ideological forces it mocks. As self-assured as the stern lawgiver whose authority he mimics, its hard to see how, short of military intervention, Wilde's disdain for his rules could ever be undone, since the power that drafts them appears to be by definition no greater than Wilde's own.

Yet in the very essay where his endorsement of idleness, usually no more expository if no less effective than an enigmatic epigram, expands to become a full-blown defense of leisure—even in "The Critic as Artist," where the taboo on labor takes on the force and compass of a cosmology as articulate as the one it opposes—Wilde submits to the categorical imperative to work. In the very essay that, gathering to itself the authority that underwrites the doctrine it reverses, inverting the hierarchal order of the Protestant ethic, hails idleness as the sign and instrument of election, condemns work as an everyday hell, and wherein the abstention from labor spells not merely social distinction, but existential salvation, Wilde, as if from a sudden failure of nerve, briefly concedes everything to the enemy.

Even with the backing of an alternate cosmology, Wilde's defense proves insufficient to stand against a rule of labor that makes no exceptions and whose agency of enforcement we will have occasion to examine again in a moment. For it is here, in the middle of his most systematic defense of indolence, that Wilde, like a deathbed convert, as if momentarily overwhelmed by a suddenly irresistible power, accepts briefly, but completely, the doctrine that he spent a good portion of his genius refuting: "Society . . . demands, and *no doubt rightly* demands, of *each* of its citizens that he should contribute some form of productive labour to the common weal, and toil and travail that the day's work may be done."[45]

---

[45] "The Critic as Artist," p. 274.

No doubt *rightly?* Since when? Like the split personality in the comedy who half of the time disavows the pleasure-driven character he embraces when he calls himself Ernest, the arch antinomian who presides over "The Critic as Artist," as if snatched by the spirit of the law that Carlyle worded, suddenly turns himself into the channel of the universal work ethic that he elsewhere disdains. As if reeducated by a regime quite opposed to the one he propagates in "The Soul of Man under Socialism," Wilde renounces absolutely the aspiration he charted there, endorsing now the ubiquity, rather than the annulment, of the compulsion to labor.

As the passage continues, the dandy recovers his voice, but only by means of a crucial compromise with an enemy now powerful enough to exact it:

> Society often forgives the criminal; it never forgives the dreamer. . . . so completely are people dominated by the tyranny of this dreadful social ideal that they are always coming shamelessly up to one at Private Views and other places that are open to the general public, and saying in a loud stentorian voice, "What are you doing?" whereas "What are you thinking?" is the only question that any single civilized being should ever be allowed to whisper to another. They mean well, no doubt, these honest beaming folk. Perhaps that is the reason they are so excessively tedious. But someone should teach them that while, in the opinion of society, Contemplation is the gravest sin of which any citizen can be found guilty in the opinion of the highest culture it is the proper occupation of man.[46]

Ditching the good-citizen act, the dandy becomes again the patrician refusnik we readily recognize, rediscovering the self-assurance that seems briefly to have abandoned him, a self-assurance sufficiently haughty to treat society, not the high one now, but rather those "honest beaming folk," with utmost condescension—"they mean well no doubt." The steadfast elitism, forgotten long enough not merely to accept, but to endorse the idea of a law that applies to everyone, returns now to dismiss such "dreadful" dogma with the confidence of a snob consummate enough to crown himself Philosopher King, and restore the ancien régime that excuses the aristocrat of high culture from the rules that apply to little people.

---

[46] Ibid., pp. 274–75.

But this is a potentate who has given Caesar his due. For now his dissent from the Protestant ethic, elsewhere as outré as Cardinal Newman's costumes, is as obscure as the sublimated essence of homosexuality that everyone suspects but no one can locate specifically in the vague ether of Hellenism that Wilde and his Oxford cronies breathed. The dandy's derogation of the general category of "action" in general has discreetly dropped any reference to work, in particular, just as his correlative defense of the "social sin" of contemplation tactfully avoids any allusion to the indolence with which it is elsewhere identified. Quietly changing the subject so as to avoid directly flouting the work ethic, the dandy takes back his bad attitude, but at the cost of giving up a good part of its edge, like the offensive entertainer who, under network pressure, tones down her show to a dimness that reveals no more than phantom of its former opposition.

I want to suggest that the agency that so magnetizes the universal commandment to labor that its enemy now bends before it is what Wilde in the essay on socialism calls the "Tyranny of Want" that compels "a great many people who, having no property of their own, and being always on the brink of sheer starvation . . . to do the work of beasts of burden, to do work that is quite uncongenial to them." For a tradition of thought at least as old as the Puritan foundations of the Protestant ethic, it isn't enough that the working class on the actual brink of it should be harrowed by the prospect of starvation. According to the most emphatic Victorian prophet of the Protestant ethic, even those who, by means of a permanent income, are sure of a dinner whether they work for it or not must be made to feel the threat of going without it if they don't. As happy to condemn the idle rich to starvation as he was the idle poor, Carlyle's vicious authoritarianism, quite unlike that of its contemporary counterpart, has at least the virtue of consistency:

> He that will not work according to his faculty, let him perish according to his necessity: there is no law juster than that. Would to Heaven one could preach it abroad into the hearts of all sons and daughters of Adam, for it is a law applicable to all; and bring it to bear, with practical obligation strict as the Poor-Law Bastille, on all! . . . That this law of "No work no recompense" should first of all be enforced on the *manual* worker, and brought stringently home to him and his numerous class, while so many other classes and persons

still go loose from it, was natural to the case. Let it be enforced there, and rigidly made good. It behooves to be enforced everywhere, and rigidly made good;—alas, not by such simple methods as "refusal of out-door relief," but by far other and costlier ones.[47]

It is the broadcast effect of what Carlyle calls the most just of laws that overwhelms Wilde's summa theologica for indolence. This law makes a slight but decisive appearance when "The Critic as Artist" describes the fate of the modern subject who aspires to the heights of classical thought, a sphere of pure thought that is at the same time the height of pure idleness:

> It is to do nothing that the elect exist. Action is limited and relative. Unlimited and absolute is the vision of him who sits at ease and watches, who walks in loneliness and dreams. But we who are born at the close of this wonderful age, are at once too cultured and too critical, too intellectually subtle and too curious of exquisite pleasures, to accept any speculations about life in exchange for life itself. To us the *citta divina* is colorless, and the *fruitio Dei* without meaning. Metaphysics do not satisfy our temperaments, and religious ecstasy is out of date. The world through which the Academic philosopher becomes "the spectator of all time and of all existence" is not really an ideal world, but simply a world of abstract ideas. When we enter it, we starve amidst the chill mathematics of thought.[48]

In the midst of an essay where the fear of going without dinner seems as inappropriate as the bill collector who briefly darkens the premises of *The Importance of Being Earnest*, the specter of starvation appears, cast to figure the fate of the modern sensibility when it enters the sphere of pure indolence: "When we enter it, we starve amidst the chill mathematics of thought." Starting with its most immediate context—why would we *starve*, rather than freeze amidst a chill?—the figure Wilde introduces here clashes with its surroundings; like the voice or suit rather too loud for society, it is slightly but distinctly out of place. It is surely a little excessive to describe

---

[47] Carlyle, *Chartism*, p. 132.
[48] "The Critic as Artist," p. 275.

even the acute alienation, not to mention the duller ennui suffered by "temperaments" "too intellectually subtle and too curious of exquisite pleasures" to be "satisfied" by the religious ecstasies and the philosophical abstractions that provided sufficient fare for our more ascetic ancestors.

Like the raised voice, really meant to reach someone out of earshot, but more like the anxiety that has floated free from its source, the lurid threat that Wilde mentions here, hard to explain by its most proximate circumstance, is better illuminated when we consider a circumstance somewhat more remote from view, namely the idleness that defines the condition of those who are subject to it. By a drift of metaphor as slight as a slip of the tongue, Wilde is made to reproduce the law whose annulment he regards as humanity's only hope; that which orders people to work or starve. And like a reaction to the raised voice, or to military maneuvers designed to intimidate those who witness them, Wilde's otherwise inexplicable submission to the doctrine of compulsory labor is best read as a response to an object lesson on the consequences of defiance, which take shape here in the shadow of starvation that falls upon the palace of the indolent.

Finally, like the conclusion drawn from a sudden awareness that the range of a bullet has no limit, Wilde's concession that the demand for labor should apply to everyone—no less odd coming from him than his concession that the demand should apply to anyone at all—may best be read as a submission to the sense that no one is excused from the continuous exertions required to avoid a universal threat. For the shadow of starvation on Wilde's social map extends beyond those who live on the actual edge of it those "who have no property of their own, and being on the brink of sheer starvation, are compelled" to work in order to get food, and are compelled to go without it when they can't; it falls as well upon those who aspire to join the elect "who exist to do nothing."

As removed from the brink of starvation as the unconscious fear of catastrophe is from the fact of it, the modern subject who aspires to the condition of classic idleness is susceptible nonetheless to a spectral emanation of the threat that Wilde, elsewhere in "The Critic as Artist," calls "the strongest, because most sordid, incentive to industry." Thus, like the police whose disciplinary operations enjoy novel extensions in a domestic literature that is formally opposed to them, the rule of labor is magnified by the offices of an essay dedicated to belittling it. For the sanction that enforces this rule is not merely reproduced in the essay; rather, by means of its sublimation there, its jurisdiction is expanded to cover even the charmed circle of those who would otherwise be immune to its powers. "[E]ven the wealthy shall not eat without working," Weber remarks, giving voice to the Puritan frame of mind that Wilde, despite his best efforts, could not keep from haunting his own.[49]

•   •   •   •   •

But as soon as the specter of starvation falls upon the region of idleness, Wilde proposes a regimen for its subject that would render this specter

[49] Weber, *The Protestant Ethic*, p. 159. The specter that haunts all leisure in Wilde's essay suggests a failure of the treaty between "an aristocratic morality of 'otium' and a puritan work ethic" that Jean Baudrillard detects in his study of conflicts correlative to the collision between the imperatives of labor and leisure that I have sought to trace. Thus, he heralds a compromise between the valorization of useless objects, and "a social morality that no more wants the object to be unemployed than the individual:"

> The functional object pretends to be decorative, it disguises itself with non-utility. . . . the futile and indolent object is charged with a practical reason. . . . objects are caught in the fundamental compromise of having to signify, that is, of having to confer social meaning and prestige in the mode of *otium* . . . and of having incidentally to submit to the powerful consensus of the democratic morality of effort, of doing. ("The Genesis of Need," in *For a Critique of the Political Economy of the Sign*, translated by Charles Levin [St. Louis: Telos Press, 1981], p. 71)

Similarly, he discerns a continuity between the demands of production and consumption, respectively associated with labor and leisure, reading them as twin aspects of a single social imperative:

> [T]he ethos of 'conspicuous' consumption is an uninterrupted performance, a stress for achievement, aiming always at providing the continual and tangible proof of social value . . . which, under inverse influences, is the heir of the principles that were the foundation of the Protestant ethic and which, according to Weber, motivated the capitalist spirit of production. The morality of consumption relays that of production, or is entangled with it in the same social logic of salvation. ("The Genesis of Need," p. 33)

But if the hostilities between the compulsion to work and the compulsion to abstain from it are suspended in a confusion of instrument and ornament, or dissolved in the long-term alliance between production and consumption, they remain, as Baudrillard notes, "fundamentally incompatible." The cooperation and convergences that take place between these forces can do nothing to quell the figure that rises on behalf of the work ethic to punish those who fail to follow its law to the letter, even if, as Baudrillard suggests, they manage, by the labor of their protestations, to sustain its spirit.

irrelevant to her again, not by inducing her to abandon her affiliation with the elect by conforming to the rule of labor, but rather by transforming her appetite and thus diminishing to the vanishing point her vulnerability to the "Tyranny of Want" that enforces this rule. In the lines that follow the revelation of its presence in the precincts of sublime idleness, Wilde introduces a program to dismantle this tyranny by means of a personal reformation that renders want tolerable rather than a social reform that would abolish it once and for all.

Like a holistic diet that concerns itself less with a low-calorie appeasement than a radical reform of appetite, Wilde answers the challenge of satisfying the modern hunger for sensuous particularities that goes unsated in the old dispensation of idleness: the hunger whose more advanced stage we have just heard called "starvation," not with a different bill of fare, but rather a different brand of desire:

> GILBERT: Who as Mr. Pater suggests somewhere, would exchange the curve of a single rose-leaf for that formless intangible Being which Plato rates so high?. . . Like Aristotle, like Goethe after he had read Kant, we desire the concrete, and nothing but the concrete can satisfy us.
>
> ERNEST: What do you propose?
>
> GILBERT: It seems to me that with the development of the critical spirit we shall be able to realize not merely our own lives, but the collective life of the race. . . . Is this impossible? I think not. By revealing to us the absolute mechanism of all action . . . the Scientific principle of Heredity has become, as it were, the warrant for the contemplative life. It has shown us that we are never less free than when we try to act. It has hemmed us round with the nets of the hunter, and written upon the wall the prophecy of our doom. . . . And yet . . . it comes to us, this terrible shadow, with many gifts in its hands, gifts of strange temperaments and subtle susceptibilities, gifts of wild ardours and chill moods of indifference. . . . And so, it is not our own life that we live, but the lives of the dead, and the soul that dwells within us is no single spiritual entity, making us personal and individual, created for our service, and entering into us for our joy. It is something that has dwelt in fearful places, and in ancient sepulcres has made its abode. It is sick with many maladies, and has memories of curious sins. It is wiser

than we are, and its wisdom is bitter. It fills us with impossible desires, and makes us follow what we know we cannot gain.[50]

What is to be done to sate our hunger for the concrete, the student asks, and Wilde's dandy, never closer to the condition of stoicism with which Baudelaire associated him, answers not directly, but rather by robbing the question of its urgency, proposing not to satisfy our longing but rather to lighten it. In place of the want whose satisfaction appears indispensable for survival, the want that is mantled in the naturalized urgency that Jean Baudrillard calls "the grace of need," the "terrible shadow" that Wilde here designates the "Scientific principle of Heredity" and "the soul that dwells within us," and whose other names we will expose in a moment, offers "impossible desires" and the inclination to "follow what we know we cannot gain," a species of yearning insatiable but also entirely bearable, interminable, but never terminal.

The state of enduring, but endurable, desire may recall the incurable nostalgia of the recovering smoker, but a more felicitous representation is Wilde's famous advertisement for the positive pleasure of the cigarette itself: "You must have a cigarette. A cigarette is the perfect type of the perfect pleasure. It is exquisite, and it leaves one unsatisfied. What more can one want?"[51] For what this preceding passage hails as "impossible desires" and the inclination to "follow what we know we cannot gain," are more than merely endurable; they are rather forms of pleasure lustrous enough to eclipse the satisfaction that would terminate them. Ranged amongst the glamorous psychological dimensionalities that Wilde designates as our inheritance, such endless desires, like the "wild ardours" and the "subtle susceptibilities" to which they are closely related, constitute the currency of our affective affluence, rather than a form of poverty that leads finally to the specter of starvation. What more can one want, at least in a society everywhere haunted by this specter? What more can the subject of this society wish for than that the lack that defines want take form as pleasure, rather than lethal need?

But if such desires are sometimes as light as the "broken heart that runs to many editions," the reformation that delivers them to us is as

---

[50] *Earnest*, pp. 275–76.
[51] *Dorian Gray*, p. 107.

harrowing as an alien abduction. While the terrible shadow that Wilde calls heredity in "The Critic as Artist" appears to "mirror" our "soul," manifests as the agent that delivers and defines our own essential genetic character, it nevertheless fills us with affects that are not our own. If the desires that this "terrible shadow" offers are "impossible" because they cannot be fulfilled, they are impossible as well because, being the desires of another, they never cease to be implausible as *our* desires.

As common, for all their strangeness, as "the tears we shed at a play," these alien desires, as light as the natural need they displace is heavy, whose endless deferral is as easy to bear as that of the other would be impossible to live with, are calculated by Wilde, with all the rhetorical resources at his disposal, as a central benefit of art. The synthetic fervors he pictures our systems absorbing belong to a genus of inorganic affects, what Wilde praises as "the exquisite sterile emotions that it is the function of Art to awaken," exquisite sterile emotions which offer a safe substitute for the potent ones they replace:

> Art does not hurt us. The tears that we shed at a play are a type of the exquisite sterile emotions that it is the function of Art to awaken. We weep but we are not wounded. We grieve, but our grief is not bitter. It is through Art, and through Art only . . . that we can shield ourselves from the sordid perils of actual existence.[52]

Frankly proposing art's "exquisite sterile emotions" as a form of prophylaxis, Wilde both enlists and revises the traditional doctrine of aesthetic disinterestedness. To admit to the region of aesthetic experience, along with the tears of the unwounded and the grief that brings no bitterness, "wild ardours" and "impossible desires" is to bend the rule of admission that Kant codified in *The Critique of Judgment*. Bend without breaking: for while Wilde populates this region with a species of affect ruled out of court by Kant, he nevertheless upholds the conception of the aesthetic as the zone where the force of that affect is transcended. For Wilde, the aesthetic experience consists in part of the category of longing excluded by the Kantian scheme—(the "interest" from which "the delight which determines the judgment of all taste" is "independent," according to Kant's

---

[52] "The Critic as Artist," pp. 273–74.

famous account, "always involves a reference to the faculty of desire")—
but it is a longing divested of its dangerous dimension, the element of
need. There is an infinite amount of desire in Wilde's more promiscuous
vision of the aesthetic experience, but it is a desire whose subject is as
immune from its vicissitudes as the disinterested one who inhabits the
more canonical grounds of the aesthetic and has succeeded in abandoning
desire altogether.[53]

Despite his most emphatic protestations, the aesthetic sphere in
The Picture of Dorian Gray proves no more immune to the hegemonic
rule of reification than it does to the judgments of popular morality and
the law. But if the idleness that high art offers, according to Wilde's measure, like the dispensation furnished by mass culture according to a familiar critique,[54] does no more than extend our engrossment in the atmosphere of alienated labor, it offers relief at least from its most dire
dimension. If the aesthetic subject, held captive as mere spectator to a
picture of the world, is no freer than her laboring counterpart from
the rigors of alienation, she is spared at least the terror by which that
regime is enforced.

But as glamorous as he makes it, the spectrum of affective color
that Wilde allows the aesthetic subject does not exactly sell itself. His enthusiasm for the alchemy that "converts an appetite into an art," the process of introjection and displacement by which organic needs give way to
impossible desires, suggests the apostolic determination to convert the
unbelieving. The determined profession of the aesthetic, the tireless promotion of "the exquisite sterile emotions that it is the function of Art to
awaken" as the material that shields us from "the sordid perils of actual

[53] Immanuel Kant, "Analytic of the Beautiful: First Moment." *The Critique of Judgment*,
translated with Analytical Indexes by James Creed Meredith (Oxford: Oxford University
Press, 1952), p. 42. The immunity that Wilde awards to aesthetic experience differs from
disinterestedness in another way, as well. Where Kant identifies disinterestedness as the character that defines the relation between the subject and object of the aesthetic, the soft desire
in Wilde's account, as good as disinterestedness, is an affect passed from the aesthetic object
to the subject.

[54] See for example, Theodor Adorno, "On the Fetish Character in Music and the Regression of Listening" in *The Essential Frankfurt School Reader*, edited with Introductions by
Andrew Arato and Eike Gebhardt (New York: Urizen Books, 1978), pp. 270–299.

existence" may put us in mind of the contemporary campaign to convince a skeptical audience that safe sex can conduct all the electric charge of risk:

> GILBERT: Yes, we can put the earth back six hundred courses and make ourselves one with the great Florentine, kneel at the same altar with him, and share his rapture and his scorn. . . . Pass on to the poem on the man who tortures himself, let its subtle music steal into your brain and colour your thoughts, and you will become for a moment what he was who wrote it. . . . We sicken with the same maladies as the poets, and the singer lends us his pain. . . . Life! Life! Don't let us go to life for our fulfillment or our experience. It is a thing narrowed by circumstances, incoherent in its utterance, and without that fine correspondence of form and spirit which is the only thing that can satisfy the artistic and critical temperament.
>
> ERNEST: Must we go, then, to Art for everything?
>
> GILBERT: For everything. Because Art does not hurt us. The tears that we shed at a play are a type of the exquisite sterile emotions that it is the function of Art to awaken. We weep but we are not wounded. . . . It is through Art, and through Art only . . . that we can shield ourselves from the sordid perils of actual existence.[55]

Judging by the force of Wilde's advertisement on their behalf, art's "exquisite sterile emotions," for all of their potence, do not invade us without support. Like the vampire, whose Paterian shadow we have already seen arise amongst them, these alien raptures must be invited to enter us. We must be persuaded to want them in.

   The triumph of yearning's benign strain in Wilde's book requires a specific act of conversion—central to Wilde's life and work: the act of conversion called seduction. This figure of seduction is easier to make out elsewhere in Wilde, but even in the passage from "The Critic as Artist" that we have already considered, it almost emerges from the shadow where it dwells there; even here we can glimpse the agent of insinuation who annuls the boundaries of our individuality by inculcating strange desires in place of our own. Its identity is intimated by the aura of seduction that surrounds "this terrible shadow, with many gifts in its hands," an aura of seduction all the brighter for the light that it borrows from the picture

---

[55] *Earnest*, pp. 273–74.

that Pater called "La Gioconda," the picture of "what in the ways of a thousand years men had come to desire."[56] Even in "The Critic as Artist," the agent who instills desire in another is difficult to distinguish from the figure desired by the other; hard not to read the desires this figure incites as desires for this figure himself.

Elsewhere, this figure of seduction is uncloseted altogether, entirely visible in all the old familiar places where the desire *of* the other is hard to tell from a desire *for* the other. We have, of course, already encountered this figure fully fledged: as "the tall, graceful young man" that Dorian Gray "could not help liking," whose "low, languid voice was absolutely fascinating." The shadow that constitutes the essential character it appears only to reveal, that incites the passions it seems merely to discover, is made flesh in the figure of Lord Henry with whom we began, Lord Henry whose insinuations conduct the exodus of Dorian Gray from the life-threatening "Tyranny of Want" to the softer genre of endurable desire; who, in an early turn in the text we have already surveyed, plots the displacement of "passions" that lead to "starvation" if left unsatisfied by a species of desire that does not.

Thus the perverse implantations that form the currency of seduction in *The Picture of Dorian Gray*, the insinuations of alien desire that work to impeach the very idea of inherent ones, is a propagation of de-essentialism that, if not certifiably strategic, is certainly convenient, and in more ways than one. If the novel's unsettling of natural desire abets a campaign to liberate perversity from the ideological shackles of a conventional heterosexism that anchors itself in an alibi of nature, it offers, as well, a route of escape from the penalties reserved for those indisposed to follow to the letter a sentence of hard labor whose end no one can predict.

[56] Walter Pater, *The Renaissance*, edited by Adam Phillips (Oxford: Oxford University Press, 1990), pp. 79–80.

SIX

OSCAR WILDE AND THE PASSION OF THE EYE

"See? I see nothing but *you*." And the truth of it had,
with this force, after a moment, so strangely lighted
his eyes that, as for pity and terror of them, she buried
her own in his breast.

—Henry James, *The Golden Bowl* (emphasis in original)

H E SEES NOTHING but her: "How beautiful is the Princess Salome tonight!"[1] Eyes as enchanted as those of the character who speaks these lines are as insensible to the warnings that would make others wince as they are blind to other sights that might distract them:

THE PAGE OF HERODIAS: You are always looking at her. You look at her too much. It is dangerous to look at people in such fashion. Something terrible may happen.
THE YOUNG SYRIAN: She is very beautiful tonight.
THE YOUNG SYRIAN: How beautiful is the Princess Salome tonight!
THE PAGE OF HERODIAS: Look at the moon.[2]

Possessed by a force of attraction that overwhelms any lunar influence as surely as it eclipses any vaguer specter of terror, these eyes are soon drawn back to the luminous figure where they lingered before. As if to the time of a metronome, except that the source of his state is a sight rather than a sound, the hypnotized soldier only thinks to repeat, moments after a concerned friend cautions against it, his vision of the astonishing spectacle: "How beautiful is the Princess tonight!" "Why do you look at her?"

---

[1] Oscar Wilde, *Salome*, [1894], in *The Major Works*, edited and with an Introduction and Notes by Isobel Murray (Oxford: Oxford University Press, 1989), p. 302. All subsequent citations of this text refer to this edition. Due to the large number of quotations in this chapter, page references will be cited in the endnotes, not in the text as in previous chapters.
[2] Ibid.

The question is as inaudible as any call to consider the cause of a compulsion, or to find a way to end it, by the ear of the one caught in its embrace. Less so, perhaps, since it seems as if the enchanted young Syrian fails to attend to the exhortations that would interrupt his gaze because he fails even to hear them, as if the magnetism of the spectacle, intensive enough to absorb all else in the field of vision, is also expansive enough to eclipse the sense of sound, as well.

Next to a gaze so engrossed, even Herod's legendary hunger for the sight of Salome seems weak by comparison. After all, Herod is not so entranced by the vision of her that he cannot see other sights, that of the young Syrian himself, for example: "[H]e was fair to look upon. He was even very fair."[3] And the vision is hardly enchanting enough to usurp the capacities of his ear. He hears loud and clear, for example, the fury of the mother's words:

> HERODIAS: You are again looking at my daughter. You must not look at her.
> I have already said so.
> HEROD: You say nothing else.[4]

And he hears, less loudly, but still clearly enough, the less canny, more frightening sounds of indistinct omens: "Do you not hear it? It is just like a beating of wings."[5]. Indeed, it is Herod's wish to be relieved from such troubling evidence of the senses that first prompts his interest in the sight of Salome: "Salome, Salome, dance for me. I pray thee dance for me. I am sad tonight. Yes, I am passing sad tonight. When I came hither I slipped in blood, which is an ill omen; also I heard in the air a beating of giant wings."[6] The expense that Herod is willing to incur for the vision tells not that he is absorbed in the spectacle, but rather how badly he wants to be.

It's difficult to say at first glance why the spectacle of Salome in particular should exert the spell that it does over the eyes of the young Syrian, since, at first glance, she seems so generic: "She is like the shadow

---

[3] Ibid., p. 312.
[4] Ibid., p. 318.
[5] Ibid., p. 313.
[6] Ibid., p. 320.

of a white rose in a mirror of silver."[7] Join the crowd. Like the routines we hear routinely enough to dull our admiration for the most celebrated wit, the young Syrian's recherché adoration will have a familiar ring to those who have read Wilde. The Princess Salome is hardly the only pretty face in town to which this formula is applied. We hear it again about Sybil Vane in *The Picture of Dorian Gray*: "A faint blush, like the shadow of a rose in a mirror of silver, came to her cheeks as she glanced at the crowded, enthusiastic house."[8] For all her star power, Salome is nonetheless part of a chorus, like those numbers that fill the book of the smooth operator who uses the same line to lure them all, a line which itself makes of the beauty that it praises no more than one amongst several likenesses, one term amongst multiple mirrorings, a mere shadow in a train of resemblances.

The luminous sight of Salome is hard to tell from the body right next to her:

THE YOUNG SYRIAN: How beautiful is the Princess Salome tonight!

THE PAGE OF HERODIAS: Look at the moon. How strange the moon seems! She is like a woman rising from a tomb. She is like a dead woman. One might fancy that she is looking for dead things.

THE YOUNG SYRIAN: She has a strange look. She is like a little princess who wears a yellow veil, and whose feet are of silver. She is like a Princess who has little white doves for feet. One might fancy she was dancing. She is like a woman who is dead. She moves very slowly.[9]

Who can trace where the figure of Salome ends and that of the moon begins? And yet who can doubt that, in the eyes entranced by her, the moon is Salome's sign, rather than the other way around? For the eyes absorbed in the sight of her, Salome's part here extends beyond the single one formally assigned to her; rather, as with the play that bears her name, the luster of her personality comprehends the entire scene. By the lights of this gaze, her luminous singularity consists of a multitude, whether it

---

[7] Ibid., p. 302.

[8] Oscar Wilde, *The Picture of Dorian Gray* [1891], in *The Major Works*, edited with an Introduction and Notes by Isobel Murray (Oxford: Oxford University Press, 1989), p. 109. All subsequent citations of this text refer to this edition.

[9] *Salome*, p. 301.

be the crowd of resemblances where the contours of her particularity are defined rather than annulled, or those that reveal themselves when the parts of her body are exposed to the pressure of the admiring eye—"Her little white hands are fluttering like doves that fly to their dovecots. They are like white butterflies. They are like white butterflies"[10]—or the population of analogies that explodes when that eye seeks to describe what it adores: "She is like a dove that has strayed. . . . She is like a narcissus trembling in the wind. . . . She is like a silver flower."[11] No wonder that the words his friend uses to warn against looking at her too much—"You look at her too much. It is dangerous to look at people in such fashion"[12]—should seem to confuse the sight of the princess with the sight of the "people"; no wonder: for if Salome is a face in the crowd, she is also, for the eye that admires her, the face *of* the crowd.

And no wonder then, that his view is so absorbed in the spectacle of Salome. What more is there to see? By his eyes, the spectacular crowd that she comprehends, slight as it is, covers the whole field of visual attraction: white roses, mirrors of silver, white butterflies, white hands fluttering like doves, a narcissus trembling in the wind, a silver flower." What are the ellipses interposed in this list but the tracks of Zeno's paradox, the marks that indicate the infinite number of points between points? Such a list may be interrupted, but how would it ever be concluded? Small as the sample is, the exquisite congeries that the young Syrian envisions in Salome bears the mark of what Benedict Anderson calls in his account of the modern census an "unbounded series,"[13] whose principle is more ostentatiously manifested in the spectacular multitudes that Salome herself sees in the "thin ivory form" of the prophet Iokanaan. Going a considerable distance to fill in the blanks unfinished by the map of the infinite spectacle that the young Syrian had begun to sketch, Salome unfolds a multitude of breathtaking sights from all over the world that, by the measure of her gaze, Iokanaan encompasses in a catalogue too long to quote in full, almost too long to read at all:

[10] Ibid., p. 305.
[11] Ibid.
[12] Ibid., p. 301.
[13] Benedict Anderson, *The Spectre of Comparisons: Nationalism, Southeast Asia, and the World* (New York: Verso, 1998), p. 29.

He is like a thin ivory statue. He is like an image of silver. . . . He is like a moonbeam, like a shaft of silver . . . his eyes . . . are like black holes burned by torches in a tapestry of Tyre. They are like the black caverns where the dragons live. . . . They are like black lakes troubled by fantastic moons . . . Iokanaan! Thy body is white, like the lilies of a field that the mower hath never mowed. Thy body is white like the snows that lie on the mountains of Judea, and come down into the valleys. . . . Thy hair is like clusters of grapes, like the clusters of black grapes that hang from the vine-trees of Edom in the land of the Edomites. Thy hair is like the cedars of Lebanon, like the great cedars of Lebanon that give their shade to the lions and the robbers who would hide them [selves] by day. . . . Thy mouth is like a band of scarlet on a tower of ivory. It is like a pomegranate cut in twain with a knife of ivory. . . . Thy mouth is like a branch of coral that fishers have found in the twilight of the sea, the coral that they keep for the kings! . . . It is like the vermilion that the Moabites find in the mines of Moab, the vermilion that the kings take from them. It is like the bow of the King of the Persians, that is painted with vermilion, and is tipped with coral.[14]

And all this infinite universe of visual splendor is encompassed by Iokanaan's "thin" form: by the measure of the gaze arrested by him, the world of visual wonder is drawn into this figures, drawn by a centripetal power that absorbs even sights from which they are distinguished: "The roses in the garden of the Queen of Arabia are not so white as thy body." By the fascinated gaze of Salome, the body whose whiteness surpasses these roses, this garden, also contains them, just as the world of doves is encircled by Salome herself in the eyes of the young Syrian: "Princess, thou who art the dove of all doves."[15] The power of compression by which all that attracts the eyes is concentrated into a single figure is sufficient to force even what is not already located there into the ocular field that it comprehends: "The long black nights, when the moon hides her face, when the stars are afraid, are not so black as thy hair. The silence that dwells in the forest is not so black."[16] All that strikes the eyes are gathered in these figures, gathered either directly, as a sight to see, or indirectly, as something witnessed

[14] *Salome*, p. 309–11.
[15] Ibid., p. 310.
[16] Ibid., p. 309.

by others, such as the vision imported through the sight "of him who cometh from a forest where he hath slain a lion, and seen gilded tigers."[17]

Sometimes a shadow haunts the spectacular multitudes that converge in the charismatic figure: that shadow is the commodity form. It hardly requires Herod's formal offer to exchange what Salome sees here for his own roster of visual pleasures to recognize that no item in this glittering multitude is any less at home than Salome herself amongst the "idol sellers": a sacred prophet in the shape of "a thin ivory statue"; "cold as ivory"; "an image of silver"; "a shaft of silver";[18] whose mouth "is like a band of scarlet on a tower of ivory"; "a pomegranate cut in twain with a knife of ivory";[19] "[her mouth is] like a branch of coral that fishers have found in the twilight of the sea, the coral that they keep for the kings!"; like "the vermilion that the Moabites find in the mines of Moab."

The commodity aspect of the items that make up this gorgeous catalogue shows up not only in their spectacular specificities, but no less in the difficulty we have preserving a view of them. Like the ennui of the decadent consumer for whom the lavish options available on an endless menu eventually come to merge—an ennui all the clearer for its contrast with the raised voice of advertisement in which they are pitched ("the coral that they keep for the kings!")—the reader's weary eye cannot keep from confusing the marvelous goods that Salome sees encompassed by the figure of Iokanaan. By the time we get to the king's ransom, who can avoid the sense that once we've seen one gorgeous thing . . . :

> I have an emerald. . . . When thou lookest through this emerald thou canst see that which passeth afar off. . . . It is the largest emerald in the whole world. Thou wilt take that, wilt thou not? . . . Salome, thou knowest my white peacocks, my beautiful white peacocks, that walk in the garden between the myrtles and the tall cypress-trees. Their beaks are gilded with gold and the grains they eat are smeared with gold, and their feet are stained with purple. When they cry out the rain comes, and the moon shows herself in the heavens when they spread their tails. Two by two they walk between the cypress-trees and the black myrtles, and each has a slave to tend it. . . . I will give thee fifty

[17] Ibid., p. 310.
[18] Ibid., p. 307.
[19] Ibid., p. 310.

of my peacocks . . . topazes yellow as . . . the eyes of tigers, opals that burn always, with a flame as cold as ice, opals that make sad men's minds, and afraid of the shadow . . . fans fashioned from the feathers of parrots.[20]

The escalating sensationalism of this list may derive from the salesman's anxious sense that he is missing the mark, but it exhibits the symptoms of a deeper malady: the restless search for novelty that seeks to outrun the shadow of sameness, whose subjective effects Simmel diagnosed as the blasé attitude, the shadow of sameness that falls upon an object world defined by a common standard that reduces all differences in quality to differences in quantity.[21] In the glittering company that surrounds us here, where the commodity takes form as a sight to see, the blasé attitude is the exhausted eye by which we recognize the auto-immune disorder that attaches itself to the society of the spectacle.

As amazing as any translation of the classic sentiment, never out of currency, *e pluribus unum*, the single silver forms of the princess and the prophet comprehend the infinite variety of the radiant screen envisioned by a capitalism that covers the globe. By this silvery light, why would the goods that Herod offers for the figure upon which she has set her eyes divert her gaze from him—as with the soldier, she appears not even to hear the words that would direct her to other sights—any more than the sight of the silvery moon would distract the young Syrian from the silver vision of Salome herself? Such sights are redundant splendor, not because they look a lot like the gorgeous goods already contained within the luminous compass where their eyes are fixed, and not because it looks as if they are already contained there, but rather because, by their lights, they really are. What array of gilded attractions could tempt these eyes from the gilded parade that already includes them all?

In any case, whatever its commercial value, anything that attracts the eyes is gathered in these figures: whether by positive or negative magnetism; whether by the soft light of the moon that the princess envelops; whether by the figure of the dead woman that she takes in, as well; whether by the exquisite beauties concentrated in the princess and

[20] Ibid., pp. 324–26.
[21] Georg Simmel, *The Philosophy of Money*, edited by David Frisby, translated by Tom Bottomore and David Frisby (London: Routledge and Kegan Paul, 1978), p. 256.

prophet, or the no less fascinating horrors that Salome counts amongst the features of Iokanaan.

> Thy body is hideous. It is like the body of a leper. It is like a plastered wall, where vipers have crawled; like a plastered wall where the scorpions have made their nest. It is like a whited sepulchre full of loathsome things. . . . Thy hair is horrible. It is covered with mire and dust. It is like a crown of thorns placed on thy head.[22]

By the calculations of the gaze so fixed upon it, all the fascinations of the visible world dwell in this body, all that excites the eye by its hideousness, all that delights it by its loveliness; by the calculations of the gaze so fixated, the prophet bears all the radiance of the One whose advent he predicts, whose violent coronation the twisted hair foreshadows, and who, by the Aesthete's devoted measure in "De Profundis," "has all the colour-elements of life."[23]

The fetishism of the gaze in *Salome* is a way of seeing practiced all over Wilde's world; it is, for example, the chief form of worship in *The Picture of Dorian Gray*, where more than one pair of eyes contract the color elements of life to a single spectacular form. There is, for example, the nearly generic actress that the young aristocrat falls for early in the story: "imagine a girl . . . with a little flower-like face, a small Greek head with plaited coils of dark-brown hair, eyes that were violet wells of passion, lips that were like the petals of a rose."[24] The difficulty we have seeing anything beyond a paint-by-numbers picture in Dorian Gray's vision of the girl he calls "the greatest romance of my life" is hardly helped by her confusion with others, princess Salome, as we have already seen, for instance, or the one that the author himself called, for a while, the greatest romance of his: "a beautiful girl called Constance Lloyd, a grave, slight, violet-eyed little Artemis, with great coils of heavy brown hair which made her flower-like head droop like a blossom."[25]

[22] *Salome*, p. 309.

[23] Oscar Wilde, "De Profundis" [1897], in *The Soul of Man and Prison Writings*, edited with an Introduction and Notes by Isobel Murray (Oxford: Oxford University Press, 1999).

[24] *Dorian Gray*, p. 85.

[25] Oscar Wilde, letter to Lily Langtry, Circa 16 December 1883. *The Letters of Oscar Wilde*, edited by Rupert Hart-Davis (New York: Harcourt, Brace & World, 1962), p. 154.

Just another showgirl to the cynical wag who has "loved so many of them,"[26] or to anyone else, for that matter, who has trouble telling apart two figures cut from the same cliché, but to the eyes of the man who adores her, she is the one who contains them all; a different role every night, she is, by these lights, also the sum of all these parts:

> She is all the great heroines of the world in one. She is more than an individual. . . . She is everything in life to me. Night after night I go to see her play. One night she is Rosalind, and the next evening she is Imogen. I have seen her die in the gloom of an Italian tomb, sucking the poison from her lover's lips. I have watched her wandering through the forest of Arden, disguised as a pretty boy in hose and doublet and dainty cap. She has been mad, and has come into the presence of a guilty king, and given him rue to wear, and bitter herbs to taste of. She has been innocent, and the black hands of jealousy have crushed her reed-like throat. I have seen her in every age and costume.[27]

The act of concentration in which Sybil Vane comes to embody the infinite variety of the theatrical spectacle is the second act of a two-part drama: the small globe whose brilliance she encompasses has already gathered to itself all the light of the city. It is all that glows in the gray world where Dorian Gray wanders the night that he meets Sybil Vane. "And where did you come across her?" Lord Henry asks:

> I will tell you, Harry, but you mustn't be unsympathetic about it. After all, it never would have happened if I had not met you. You filled me with a wild desire to know everything about life. For days after I met you, something seemed to throb in my veins. As I lounged in the Park, or strolled down Piccadilly, I used to look at everyone who passed me, and wonder, with a mad curiosity, what sort of lives they led. Some of them fascinated me. Others filled me with terror. There was an exquisite poison in the air. I had a passion for sensations. . . . Well, one evening about seven o'clock, I determined to go out in search of some adventure. I felt that this gray, monstrous London of ours, with its myriads of people, its sordid sinners, and its splendid sins . . . must have something in store for me. I fancied a thousand things. The mere danger gave me a sense of delight. I remembered what you had said to me on that

[26] *Dorian Gray,* p. 45.
[27] Ibid., pp. 44, 47.

wonderful evening when we first dined together, about the search for beauty being the real secret of life. I don't know what I expected, but I went out and wandered eastward, soon losing my way in a labyrinth of grim streets and black, grassless squares.[28]

Amongst the sensations promised by "this grey, monstrous London of ours, with its myriads of people, its sordid sinners, and its splendid sins," one form is notably lacking: the prospect of sensations that meet the eye, dim to begin with, is quite shut out by the time Dorian Gray wanders eastward, losing his way "in a labyrinth of grim streets and black, grassless squares." And well before the city itself turns dark, the visual element of the crowds Dorian Gray encounters has already been eclipsed: "I used to look at everyone who passed me, and wonder, with a mad curiosity, what sort of lives they led." Not content with the calmer pleasure of just looking at the faces in the crowd, Dorian Gray has a "mad curiosity" to know what lies beneath the surface of sight. The pupil here departs from the eyes of his teacher, for whom the mere sight of the urban masses is sensation enough. "All I want now is to look at life,"[29] Lord Henry remarks as he prepares for his walk through London, a walk that follows the wandering footsteps of the most celebrated city sightseer: "The masses had become so much a part of Baudelaire that it is rare to find a description of them in his works. His most important subjects are hardly ever encountered in descriptive form. As Dujardin so aptly put it, he was 'more concerned with implanting the image in the memory than with adorning and elaborating it.' "[30]

No such illumination from the masses is available to the vision of one for whom all sinners are gray, for whom the dazzling glare of the theater is like a sudden dawn to an eye grown accustomed to the dark:

About half-past eight I passed by an absurd little theatre, with great flaring gas-jets and gaudy playbills. A hideous Jew, in the most amazing waistcoat I ever beheld in my life, was standing at the entrance, smoking a vile cigar. He had greasy ringlets, and an enormous diamond blazed in the centre of a soiled shirt. . . . he took off his hat with an air of gorgeous servility. . . . You will

[28] Ibid., p. 83–84.
[29] Ibid., p. 80.
[30] Walter Benjamin, "On Some Motifs in Baudelaire," in *Illuminations*, translated by H. Zohn (New York: Schocken, 1969), pp. 167–68.

130

laugh at me, I know, but I really went in and paid a whole guinea for the stage-box. To the present day I can't make out why I did so.[31]

Why not? What else is there to see in town? As if by some miracle of urban planning, or some ruin or blank of the eye, all the color elements of London have been concentrated in this theater, as if the "blaze" of an "enormous diamond" condenses all its light; as if, assuming his customary role as scapegoat, the "hideous Jew" with his "amazing waistcoat" is inducted to stand for all that is there to fascinate vision with its ugliness. Entering the theater, this contraction of the eyes is completed with the sight of Sybil Vane who, like a princess, like a prophet, gathers within herself the infinite variety of the only show around.

And here the modern "idolatry" of the gaze in *Dorian Gray*—both the fetishism of his own eyes and, as we will see now, the fetishism of the eyes for him—differs from its Old Testament correlative: the infinite fields of light taken in by the luster of the charismatic in *Salome* gives way to the specific fields taken in by his modern embodiment. Thus the radiance of Sybil Vane reaches no further than the radius of the theater. The artist who "sees everything" in Dorian Gray himself actually sees no further than the dimensions of his canvas, ample enough to contain all that interests his eye: " 'He is all my art to me now,' said the painter gravely. . . . I paint from him, draw from him, sketch from him. . . . I see everything in him."[32]

And where the vision of Dorian Gray fails to absorb the field of art, as he does for the painter of the portrait, he displaces it, as he does the portrait itself. This usurpation is evident amongst the lower orders of the industry: the "rough-looking young assistant" of a "celebrated framemaker" "had never seen anyone so marvelous" and his more jaundiced employer, "whose admiration for art was considerably tempered by the inveterate impecuniosity of most of the artists who dealt with him," admires instead the vision of Dorian Gray. "As a rule he never left his shop. . . . But he always made an exception in favour of Dorian Gray. There

[31] *Dorian Gray*, p. 84.
[32] Ibid., p. 55.

was something about Dorian Gray that charmed everybody. It was a pleasure even to see him."[33] A faculty for disinterested interest, a capacity to be attracted to what is beautiful for its own sake, an aesthetic sensitivity as rusty in the small businessman of art as the susceptibilities of young love in the middle aged, is elevated and made keen again by the picture of Dorian Gray.

This takeover of the aesthetic, witnessed when the mere joy of seeing him revives the profitless attraction traditionally reserved as the provenance of art, also occurs as well through more finely filtered lenses of visual pleasure:

> Lord Henry looked at him. Yes, he was certainly wonderfully handsome, with his finely-curved scarlet lips, his frank blue eyes, his crisp gold hair. There was something in his face that made one trust him at once. All the candour of youth was there, as well as all youth's passionate purity. One felt that he had kept himself unspotted from the world. . . . Grace was his, and the white purity of boyhood, and beauty such as old Greek marbles kept for us.[34]

The rumor of an apostolic succession arranged by the ambiguity of these lines, an apostolic succession in which the beauty kept by Greek marbles is passed on to Dorian Gray himself, and which takes part in a broader act of investiture through which a boy, who just a few lines before was no more than "some gracious form," assumes the title to the entire category—"Grace is *his*": an act of investiture through which Dorian Gray comes to possess all the luster of the categories for which he furnishes the outward and visible sign. "Grace is *his*"; "*[a]ll* the candour of youth was there, as well as *all* youth's passionate purity"; "*all* the passion of the romantic spirit"; "*all* the spirit that is Greek."

The miscellaneous characters who constitute it—a nervous artist, a stolid merchant, a dispassionate aristocrat—suggest the broad growth in the population of admirers that takes place when, in the spirit of modernity, the field of visual attraction comprehended by the charismatic figure is divided into specialized sectors. If the breadth of these subfields falls short of the infinite universe that the charismatic comprehends in the eyes

---

[33] Ibid., pp. 137, 139.
[34] Ibid., pp. 59–60.

of "Salome," the vision that so perceives the charismatic at the same time expands from a single, singular subjectivity to a larger consensus that defines the art world, or the coterie of fashion: "His mode of dressing, and the particular styles that from time to time he affected, had their marked influence on the young exquisites of the Mayfair balls and Pall Mall club windows, who copied him in everything that he did, and tried to reproduce the accidental charm of his graceful, though to him only half-serious, fopperies."[35]

The tribute that the fashion world pays to its model—unlike the idolatry of the artist, or the "look of shy wonder" in the assistant's stolen glance, or even the unspoken admiration of the subtle aesthete—has a certain edge to it, the competitive edge present whenever the desire to be like someone else is put in play. Not in their wildest dreams would Basil Hallward, the rough-looking young assistant, or even Lord Henry imagine that they could look like the figure splendid enough to comprehend the vision of art. But the admiration that lights the eyes of the young exquisites of the Mayfair balls and Pall Mall club windows as well includes the ambitious glare of emulation. Thus the young men who see a model in Dorian Gray at once affirm and endanger his monopoly over the visual field that concerns them. On one hand, to acknowledge him as a model is to hail him as the subject supposed to know the right look; on the other, the effort of imitation by which they recognize him as such menaces the franchise he holds with the threat of dissemination, a threat delivered sotto voce in the form of a cruel aphorism: "Even the disciple has his uses. He stands behind one's throne, and at the moment of one's triumph whispers in one's ear that, after all, one is immortal."[36]

But Dorian Gray is as much indemnified against the down-market brand of immortality, where charisma gives way to a retail line, as he is indemnified against the mortality with whose ravages the novel is famously obsessed. He is encircled by a force of exclusion that, like the most vigilant security guard, is ready to repel the slightest shadow of trespass cast on the spotlight of the star, and that exerts itself even in the novel's first lines

---

[35] Ibid., p. 144.
[36] Wilde, "A Few Maxims for the Instruction of the Over-Educated," in *Major Works*, p. 571.

to protect the story's mise-en-scène. As if disinclined to abide, even at some distance away, even for the length of a sentence, the most insignificant distraction from the sight at the center of the room, this force as I remarked in chapter 3 arranges the disappearance of the only other person near the stage the very moment he is introduced: "In the center of the room, clamped to an upright easel, stood the full length portrait of a young man of extraordinary personal beauty, and in front of it, some little distance away, was sitting the artist himself, whose sudden disappearance some years ago caused, at the time, such public excitement."[37]

The protective tendency, visible even in such slight turns of syntax, to remove from view anyone who might cohabit the field of light with Dorian Gray is full-blown when it comes to those who would imitate him in the sphere of fashion. For while the young exquisites may try to reproduce the accidental charm of his graceful, though to him only half-serious fopperies, they don't even come close. Indeed, quite to the contrary: the very effort to emulate him is murder on the looks. Chief amongst the toxic properties of the "wonderful influence of Dorian Gray" "so fatal to young men," is a cosmetic disaster impossible to separate from the other catastrophes that result from the effort to follow him. "What about Adrian Singleton, and his dreadful end" in an opium den,[38] "[a] young man with smooth yellow hair" lost amongst "crouching Malays," "[t]he twisted limbs, the gaping mouths, the staring lustreless eyes," his own "bending" body already adapting the habits of the environment into which he has disappeared?[39] (Like other upper-crust renegades, the crimes of this reprobate stop short of class treason: disappearing from public view, Adrian Singleton has at least the social sense to heed the rule of Wilde's set, which defines the body it is "a "pleasure to see" as the only one fit to be seen.) Bent now, like the twisted limbs that surround him, the body of Adrian Singleton reaches the bitter end of those moved by the example of Dorian Gray: an end as ironic as the aphorist's most lethal punch line; the ugly end of those who seek to emulate the most beautiful figure in town; the ugly end that leaves the most beautiful figure in town the only one left

[37] *The Picture of Dorian Gray*, p. 49.
[38] Ibid., p. 159.
[39] Ibid., p. 188.

134

standing there. Like the undeniable damage done to the complexion by most known recreational drugs, the high life that Dorian Gray takes up and, along with "the accidental charm of his graceful, though to him only half-serious, fopperies," he drives others to take up as well, destroys the appearance of anybody whose immune system falls short of the full coverage provided by his own. When, near the end of the story, Lord Henry tells Dorian Gray of yet another "very young man" who "has already copied your neckties, and has begged me to introduce him to you,"[40] we know that the novel is preparing us for his death, consoling us in advance with the prospect of at least one complexion saved, one doubtless as pure as that of the milkmaid he chooses to spare himself.

And the portrait, "what about [its] dreadful end?"—the portrait swayed by the same tide of influence that draws Dorian Gray's enchanted minions to "cop[y] him in everything that he did," and thus condemned to an exile beyond the pale of public view,

> A feeling of pain crept over him as he thought of the desecration that was in store for the fair face on the canvas. . . . Was it to alter with every mood to which he yielded? Was it to become a monstrous and loathsome thing, to be hidden away in a locked room, to be shut out from the sunlight that had so often touched to brighter gold the waving wonder of its hair? The pity of it! The pity of it!
>
> For a moment he thought of praying that the horrible sympathy that existed between him and the picture might cease. It had changed in answer to a prayer; perhaps in answer to a prayer it might remain unchanged. And yet, who, that knew anything about Life, would surrender the chance of remaining always young, however fantastic that chance might be, or with what fateful consequences it might be fraught? Besides was it really under his control? Had it indeed been prayer that had produced the substitution? Might there not be some curious scientific reason for it all? If thought could exercise its influence upon a living organism, might thought exercise an influence upon dead and inorganic things? Nay, without thought or conscious desire, might not things external to ourselves vibrate in unison with our moods and passions, atom calling to atom in secret love or strange affinity? But the reason

---

[40] Ibid., p. 210.

was of no importance. He would never again tempt by a prayer any terrible power. If the picture was to alter, it was to alter. That was all. Why inquire too closely into it.[41]

We hear Dorian Gray defend himself in the same terms when Basil Hallward confronts him with the hideous fate of those who have fallen under the spell of his influence; defends himself with the same assertion that such ruin is not "under his control": "You ask me about Henry Ashton and young Perth. Did I teach the one his vices, and the other his debauchery. . . . am I [their] keeper?"[42]

But we hear more than that in this passage. For a moment, we are invited to imagine Dorian Gray as a model for more than the young men he encounters, for more than the picture, which, by "secret love or strange affinity," is driven to mirror him; for a moment we are invited to imagine Dorian Gray as a model for anyone who would seek to have the youth that is beauty in and beyond Wilde's world; for a moment we are invited to imagine that the subject of this sentence—"And yet, who, that knew anything about Life, would surrender the chance of remaining always young"—is the picture itself, rather than Dorian Gray. For a moment, we are invited to imagine that Dorian Gray's studied indifference in the face of the fate of those who, for "secret love or strange affinity," seek to reflect him is like the vacant look of the model trained to indifference about the "external things" that would, through no "thought or conscious desire" of his own, "vibrate in unison" with him.

However brief, the induction of Dorian Gray as the model of models becomes him, at least by the dark view of the fashion world's discontents: the fate of those external things that seek to imitate him bends to the spirit of melodrama an everyday path of disillusionment routinely traced by those who would venture upon the runway of glamour. For the dilemma of those who follow the footsteps of the figure they hail as the visible symbol of grace, only to find themselves cast out entirely from the circle of light that he comprehends, extends beyond the victims

[41] Ibid., pp. 126–27.
[42] Ibid., p. 160.

of fashion in *The Picture of Dorian Gray*, social corpses like Adrian Single-ton or the portrait itself, only waiting to get themselves buried. It includes, as well, the disappointment, for some no less mortifying, that arises when-ever the spell of identification is broken—perhaps, as for the dwarf in the fairy tale, broken by the sight in the mirror we see in private—the spell of identification which is the very sense of fashion and coaxes us to see our own bodily ego reflected, as if by a mirror of silver, in the figure of glamour.

The pathetic end of the external things that would emulate Do-rian Gray thus accords with a familiar arraignment of the culture industry as mass opiate, casting its attractions as so many projections of a specious availability, so many fantasies that the lifestyles of the rich and famous are made to fit us all. For it is only his deluded admirers, and more specifically those of them with the money and inclination for his neckties, who could imagine that his look could be knocked off: Dorian Gray proves with a vengeance that he is inimitable in the end. His potential rivals disqualified from the field of visual attraction by their very effort to join him there, Dorian Gray keeps to himself all the glamour that he appears merely to exemplify. For the "many, especially among the very young men, who saw, or fancied that they saw, in Dorian Gray, the true realization of a type of which they had often dreamed,"[43] such impregnable grace is all that the world has to offer of what the eye would care to see.

• • • • •

No wonder that eyes so enamored can hardly tear themselves away from the sight of someone like this; that the artist who sees everything in Do-rian Gray must see him "[e]very day"; that the stage-struck youth watches Sybil Vane every night; that the young Syrian can't take his eyes off Salome to save his life; that the eyes of Salome herself are no less captive to the sight of Iokanaan: "I would look closer at him. . . . I must look at him closer."[44] (For all its gaudy ferocity, Salome's famous revenge against Ioka-naan has its origins in the pedestrian humiliation of one who cannot help but look at the other who recognizes, but disdains, her gaze: "The arm of

[43] Ibid., p. 155.
[44] *Salome*, p. 308.

137

the Executioner, comes forth . . . bearing on a silver shield the head of Iokanaan. Salome seizes it. . . . Ah! wherefore didst thou not look at me, Iokanaan?"[45]

And no wonder that the gaze that bestows upon the prophet a crown of thorns wreathes him as well with a necklace of serpents: "Thy hair . . . is like a crown of thorns placed on thy head. It is like serpents coiled round thy neck"; no wonder that the figure who thrills vision with all the elements that attract the eye makes way for the one who turns the fascinated gaze into the frozen stare. Of course, the agony of the arrested eye in the story of Medusa, at least at first glance, is more excruciating than it is in Wilde; instead of their transformation into stone, such eyes are subject to what, at first glance, seems the incomparably milder mortification of mere exposure. The fixated gaze is helpless to avert his eyes when the charismatic figure confronts him face to face: "SALOME [*Looking at the young Syrian*]: Ah!"[46] The "terrible thing" that will result from too much looking at her begins with just this turnabout—the one canonized in the classic reverse-shot where the voyeur, entrapped more by the pleasure of watching than by the temporary paralysis of the legs that gives that pleasure its occasion, is suddenly exposed to the eye of the subject he had been eyeing himself.

But the vulnerability of the gaze to this reversal, the "being-seen-by-another" that Sartre defines as "the truth of 'seeing-the-Other,' " is attended by its own anxieties: "What I apprehend immediately when I hear the branches crackling behind me is not that *there is someone there*; it is that I am vulnerable, that I have a body which can be hurt, that I occupy a place and that I can not in any case escape from the space in which I am without defense—in short that I *am seen*."[47] The exposure of the gaze, which Sartre casts as the occasion for the existential unease that arises from our own vulnerability to other people, merges in and beyond the work of Oscar Wilde with the exposure of something particular in the gaze, the passion of the eye that Basil Hallward diagnoses as a "curious artistic idolatry":

[45] Ibid., p. 328.
[46] Ibid., p. 306.
[47] Jean Paul Sartre, "The Existence of Others," in *Being and Nothingness*, translated and with an Introduction by Hazel E. Barnes (New York: Washington Square Press, 1956) p. 347 (emphasis added).

"[W]hy won't you exhibit his portrait?" asked Lord Henry.

"Because, without intending it, I have put into it some expression of all this curious artistic idolatry, of which, of course, I have never cared to speak to him. He knows nothing about it. He shall never know about it. But the world might guess it; and I will not bare my soul to their shallow, prying eyes. My heart shall never be put under their microscope."[48]

The overly interested gaze of the artist, all but announced by the picture, which worships the comely form it paints as an idol, even the less lurid gaze that is remarkably, and therefore excessively, curious, is all that it takes to recognize the interest of its subject's heart.

To avoid such exposure, elaborate efforts are undertaken in Wilde, efforts that end, as we will see, with eyes as hard as those transformed by the Gorgon's head, and that begin with the artist's efforts to protect his gaze from the glance of others by casting his not directly at Dorian Gray, but rather, like a figure in a mirrored shield, at his image in the remote region of art:

Dorian, from the moment I met you . . . I was dominated, soul, brain, and power by you. You became to me the visible incarnation of that unseen ideal whose memory haunts us artists like an exquisite dream. I worshiped you. I grew jealous of every one to whom you spoke. I wanted to have you all to myself. I was only happy when I was with you. When you were away from me you were still present in my art. . . . Of course I never let you know anything about this. . . . You would not have understood it. I hardly understood it myself. I only knew that I had seen perfection face to face. . . . Weeks and weeks went on, and I grew more and more absorbed in you. Then came a new development. I had drawn you as Paris in dainty armour, and as Adonis with huntsman's cloak and polished boar-spear. Crowned with heavy lotus-blossoms you had sat on the prow of Adrian's barge, gazing across the green turbid Nile. You had leant over the still pool of some Greek woodland, and seen in the water's silent silver the marvel of your own face. And it had all been as art should be, unconscious, ideal and remote.[49]

[48] *Dorian Gray*, p. 56.
[49] Ibid., pp. 132–33.

All the familiar pains of a love that dare not speak its name, one that dare not in the drama of ocular proof we are observing here; Basil Hallward avoids giving himself away to the man he worships by avoiding eye contact with him. Dorian Gray, caught up in his own reflection, taken up with a long view, or engaged wholly in his task as spectacle, is "unconscious" of, "remote" from, the gaze that is trained on him. Unconscious of that gaze because he is remote from it: "And it had all been what art should be, unconscious, ideal, and remote." The distraction of the young man's glance in these pictures exhibits the blindness that defines the condition of any painted figure, none of whom are after all in a position to look back upon the eye fixed on them, any more so than the "seventeen photographs" that Lord Henry keeps of Dorian Gray, unbeknownst to the subject himself.[50]

But even the visual pleasure that can be enjoyed when its subject is so unconscious can never be free from the fear of exposure, a fear which begins with the painter's first look at the picture of Dorian Gray:

> As the painter looked at the gracious and comely form he had so skillfully mirrored in his art, a smile of pleasure passed across his face, and seemed about to linger there. But he suddenly started up, and, closing his eyes, placed his fingers upon the lids, as though he sought to imprison within his brain some curious dream from which he feared he might awake.[51]

Why, all of a sudden, is there a pressing need to imprison within his brain as a "curious dream" the image that is after all still right in front of him? Could it be that the sudden start that interrupts the joy of his gaze is connected to the disappearance here of the mediating term that provides the saving distance between seer and seen? Could it be that his mirroring is skillful enough to remove all traces of itself, and that the painter is therefore looking not at the painting of the "gracious and comely" form, but rather at the very life that it represents, which, unlike the picture, could look back at him? (After all, the aesthetic alchemy by which a work of art is confused for the human form it represents is a regular event on Wilde's fictional calendar, both in and beyond the miraculous moment in

[50] Ibid., p. 81.
[51] Ibid., p. 49.

The Picture of Dorian Gray). As classic in its own way as the philosophical impulse to enshrine in thought the image of the comely form is the possibility of embarrassment that may well provoke this impulse here, the possibility that the watcher may feel that he is watched himself, whether by the comely form that he gazes upon suddenly come to life, or another person in the room, there all along, who announces himself in the next sentence: "'It is your best work, Basil, the best thing you have ever done,' said Lord Henry, languidly."[52]

And even in the absence of any eyes trained directly on the painter, anyone who looks at his picture can see perfectly well what he calls his "curious artistic idolatry." Thus, Basil Hallward confesses it to Dorian Gray only because he is certain that he has already seen it himself:

> One day, a fatal day I sometimes think, I determined to paint a wonderful portrait of you as you actually are, not in the costume of dead ages, but in your own dress and in your own time. Whether it was the realism of the method, or the mere wonder of your personality, thus directly presented to me without mist or veil, I cannot tell. But I know that as I worked at it, every flake and film of colour seemed to me to reveal my secret. I grew afraid that others would know of my idolatry. I felt, Dorian, that I had told too much, that I had put too much of myself into it. Then it was that I resolved never to allow the picture to be exhibited.[53]

The picture of Dorian Gray "without mist or veil" brings into play again the rumor that the comely form reflected in it has come to life and that the "face to face" contact with it, which the artist had sought to consign to an inaccessible past by means of the painting or, in the preceding passage, the pluperfect tense ("I only knew that I *had seen* perfection face to face"), is suddenly a present danger. But even after we dismiss as an optical illusion the prospect of a subject no longer able to do so returning the gaze of the eyes that adore him, these eyes are quite exposed nonetheless. By depicting "a young man of extraordinary personal beauty" "without mist or veil," the artist does the same to himself, like those photographers

---

[52] Ibid.
[53] Ibid., p. 133.

whose images are so many contemporary reproductions of the picture of Dorian Gray, and whose sexual preferences no one could doubt.

But even concealing the picture isn't sufficient to protect the gaze that is exposed there from prosecution and punishment far surpassing the usual measures in such cases. The sentence usually imposed upon the arrested eye—no more, or less, by common guidelines, than the silent retaliations of the confused, contemptuous, or hostile counterglance—are enhanced for Basil Hallward, as they are for the spoiled prince in Wilde's fairy tale, about whom "[m]any curious stories" of conspicuous scopophilia were related. "[H]e was "caught sight of . . . kneeling in real adoration before a great picture that had just been brought from Venice"; "He had passed a whole night in noting the effect of the moonlight on a silver image of Endymion":

> And as he slept he dreamed a dream. . . . He thought that he was standing in a long, low attic, amidst the whir and clatter of many looms. . . .
>
> The young King went over to one of the weavers, and stood by him and watched him.
>
> And the weaver looked at him angrily and said, "Why art thou watching me?"[54]

In the case of Basil Hallward, the amplification of the penalty suffered by the exposed gaze is still more severe. A reader as overwrought and accurate as Basil Hallward himself may see his death as a vigilante-style execution, a murderous entrapment in which the painter is set up to get caught looking as he gazes, yet again, at the picture of Dorian Gray:

> It was some foul parody, some infamous, ignoble satire. . . . Still, it was his own picture. . . . He turned, and looked at Dorian Gray with the eyes of a sick man. . . . The young man was leaning against the mantel-shelf, watching him with that strange expression that one sees on the faces of those who are absorbed in a play. . . . There was simply the passion of the spectator, with perhaps a flicker of triumph in his eyes. A flicker of triumph that sparks into violence when Dorian Gray leaps into action to avenge the object of the artist's gaze: Dorian Gray glanced at the picture, and suddenly an uncontrollable

---

[54] Oscar Wilde, "The Young King," in *Complete Shorter Fiction*, edited with an Introduction by Isobel Murray (Oxford: Oxford University Press, 1995), pp. 172, 175.

feeling of hatred for Basil Hallward came over him, as though it had been suggested to him by the image on the canvas. . . . He rushed at him, and dug the knife into the great vein behind the ear.[55]

No less harrowing than the fate of those destroyed in the Greek myth, the suffering of the arrested gaze in *The Picture of Dorian Gray* is hardly confined to the late-Victorian closet drama. Who but the most culturally innocent or willfully blind could fail to see that the specter of such terror haunts those less gothic practices of everyday aversion, by means of which the eye avoids getting caught looking, as much as dim memories of other terrors help to prevent all sorts of passions from exposing themselves?

• • • • •

How can the arrest of the eye that brings all this risk be brought to an end? Only when the field of visual attraction concentrated in the charismatic is dispersed, his power dismantled, and the eye engrossed there thus freed. Such a dispersal takes place the night that Sybil Vane disentangles herself from "the shadows" of others, the night that her performance becomes "absolutely self contained"—"It was not nervousness. Indeed, so far from being nervous, she was absolutely self-contained. . . . She was a complete failure." Sybil Vane abandons not only the crowd that admired her performance on stage, but also the crowd of shadows that she embodied there, and thus commits the indiscretion that Simmel describes as the "danger" that intimacy poses for the dyad where it is housed: "It leads them to consider what they share with others and what perhaps is the most important part of their personalities—objective, intellectual, generally interesting, generous features as lying outside the marital relation; and thus they gradually eliminate it from their marriage."[56]

"What have I to do with the puppets of a play?" For the man who adores the sight of her, the answer is everything: "You have killed my love. You used to stir my imagination. Now you don't even stir my curiosity. You simply produce no effect. I loved you because you . . . realized the dreams of great poets and gave shape and substance to the shadows of

[55] *Dorian Gray,* p. 163.
[56] Ibid., pp. 109–10.

art. . . . Without your art you are nothing. . . . What are you now? A third-rate actress with a pretty face."[57] Abjuring the magic by which she encompassed all the light of the theater, Sybil Vane rejoins the chorus. Prompted by the desire to separate herself from the spectacular crowd that she comprehended, Sybil Vane only succeeds in disappearing into it.

And as the spectacle he worshiped recedes into the crowd, the crowd itself gradually takes on the luster that had been concentrated in her charisma:

> "I am going," he said at last, in his calm, clear voice. "I don't wish to be unkind, but I can't see you again. You have disappointed me." . . . Where he went he hardly knew. He remembered wandering through dimly lit streets, past gaunt black-shadowed archways and evil-looking houses. Women with hoarse voices and harsh laughter had called after him. Drunkards had reeled by cursing, and chattering to themselves like monstrous apes. He had seen grotesque children huddled upon doorsteps, and heard shrieks and oaths from gloomy courts.
>
> As the dawn was just breaking he found himself close to Covent Garden. The darkness lifted, and, flushed with faint fires, the sky hollowed itself into a perfect pearl. Huge carts filled with nodding lilies rumbled slowly down the polished empty street. The air was heavy with the perfume of the flowers, and their beauty seemed to bring him an anodyne for his pain. He followed into the market, and watched the men unloading their wagons. A white-smocked carter offered him some cherries. He thanked him, wondered why he refused to accept any money for them, and began to eat them listlessly. They had been plucked at midnight, and the coldness of the moon had entered into them. A long line of boys carrying crates of striped tulips, and of yellow and red roses, defiled in front of him, threading their way through the huge jade-green piles of vegetables. Under the portico, with its grey sun-bleached pillars, loitered a troop of draggled bareheaded girls, waiting for the auction to be over. Others crowded round the swinging doors of the coffee-house in the Piazza. The heavy cart horses slipped and stamped upon the rough stones, shaking their

[57] Georg Simmel, "The Isolated Individual and the Dyad," in *The Sociology of Georg Simmel*, translated, edited, and with an Introduction by Kurt H. Wolff (New York: The Free Press, 1950), p. 127.

144

bells and trappings. Some of the drivers were lying asleep on a pile of sacks. Iris-necked, and pink-footed the pigeons ran about picking up seeds.

After a little while, he hailed a hansom, and drove home. For a few moments he loitered upon the doorstep, looking round at the silent Square with its blank close-shuttered windows, and its staring blinds. The sky was pure opal now, and the roofs of the houses glistened like silver against it. From some chimney opposite a thin wreath of smoke was rising. It curled, a violet riband, through the nacre-coloured air.[58]

Here, the figure of the crowd is raised, healed, purified, and made lustrous; Assuming the brilliance of the girl who has faded into a crowd herself, "those white silent people we call the dead," the now radiant city even seems to bear traces of Sybil Vane. Even the sound of her voice—"the tremulous ecstasy just before dawn"—is recalled in the scene of this radiance, but it is the vision of the girl whose disseminated effects may be sighted in the crowds that Dorian Gray encounters. In "a long line of boys carrying crates of stripped tulips, and of yellow and red roses," he glimpses something like the vision of flowers that he saw in her face, "a little flower-like face and lips . . . like the petals of a rose." The "iris-necked pigeons" resemble her "reed-like throat," and the "roofs of houses" whose reflections of the dawn "glisten like silver" the mirror of silver absorbed by her blush. In the jewelled light of the sky and the "staring blinds" in the "silent Square" that watch it, there is a luster like the one concentrated in the girl whom Dorian Gray proposes to raise on a pedestal, but only because, to him, she is higher than that already, "divine beyond all living things," and especially beyond her audience, in the "absurd theater" where she appears, the "common, rough people, with their coarse faces and brutal gestures," who "sit silently and watch her."

And as the figure of the crowd is raised up, Dorian Gray gains an eye for it. At first he is as insensible to it as the staring blinds: unconscious wanderings through "dimly-lit streets, past gaunt black-shadowed archways" "evil-looking houses" ("Where he went, he hardly knew), give way to sense enough (although not the sense of sight yet) to receive as "anodyne for his pain" the "beauty" of the flowers that fill the vendors' carts,

---

[58] *Dorian Gray,* p. 113.

sense enough to feel at least the coldness of fruit if not to observe its lunar source. Finally, though, he is inclined to see the "the silent Square with its blank close-shuttered windows, and its staring blinds. The sky was pure opal now, and the roofs of the houses glistened like silver": finally, his vision of the crowd is awakened as he "loiters [to look] at it upon the doorstep."

This lingering lasts "only for a few moments" before Dorian Gray turns in: as the field of visual attraction breaks free from the narrow region of the theater that Sybil Vane comprehended, and disperses itself in the crowds of the city, the gaze of the subject who sees all this luster is casual about any single sight. Floating now through a world where the brilliance concentrated in the stage spectacle has been dispersed into the lights of the common multitude, Dorian Gray is disposed again to the ephemeral encounters that his teacher sought to inculcate all along, in which the "perfect point of rose-coloured joy" that is his spectacular kiss with Sybil Vane is released and disseminated into a thousand points of briefer pleasure. Thus after the first romance of his life, Dorian Gray adheres in the sphere of the visual, and in all other spheres as well, to the rule of promiscuity that is the only tendency promulgated by the school of Lord Henry, never repeating the indiscretion that he commits with Sybil Vane, "the error of arresting [one's] . . . development by any formal acceptance of creed or system, or of mistaking, for a house in which to live, an inn that is but suitable for the sojourn of a night";[59] a creed or system like marriage, a house like the home where its adherents are assigned to live: "I hope that Dorian Gray will make this girl his wife, passionately adore her for six months, and then suddenly become fascinated by some one else"; "As for marriage, of course that would be silly, but there are other and more interesting bonds between men and women. I will certainly encourage them. They have the charm of being fashionable."[60]

Fast on the heels of his affair with Sybil Vane, and as if to make up for the time he lost with her, Dorian Gray indulges his desire to "know everything of life" with enough concentration to pulverize all sense of narrative continuity, enough to divert the hero from the path of progress

[59] Ibid., pp. 113–14.
[60] Ibid., p. 146.

146

and to wander instead with only the dimmest sense of aim through a crowd of attractions as dense as an epic forest or urban center. But as with other ecstatic experiences or episodes of error, what looks like a wrong turn or a lost weekend turns out to be a stage of development key to the career of the protagonist. For in the practically unreadable chapter where he appears to do nothing but drift for years from booth to booth in a global arcade, whose spectacular immensity lights up even the darkest places and times, Dorian Gray consolidates the habit of visual promiscuity that replaces the charismatic spectacle:

> And so he would now study perfumes. . . . He saw that there was no mood of the mind that had not its counterpart in the sensuous life, and set himself to discover their true relations, wondering what there was . . . in ambergris that stirred one's passions, and in violets that woke the memory of dead romances, and in musk that troubled the brain, and in champak that stained the imagination. . . . At another time he devoted himself entirely to music, and in a long latticed room, with a vermilion-and-gold ceiling and walls of olive-green lacquer, he used to give curious concerts in which mad gypsies tore wild music from little zithers, or grave yellow-shawled Tunisians plucked at the strained strings of monstrous lutes, while grinning negroes beat monotonously upon copper drums, and, crouching upon scarlet mats, slim turbaned Indians blew through long pipes of reed or brass. . . . Yet after some time, he wearied of them, and would sit in his box at the Opera . . . listening in rapt pleasure to "Tannhauser". . . . On one occasion he took up the study of jewels. . . . The taste enthralled him for years. . . . He would often spend a whole day settling and resettling in their cases the various stones he collected, such as the olive-green chrysoberyl that turns red by lamplight, the cymophane with its wire-like line of silver, the pistachio-coloured peridot, rose-pink and wine-yellow topazes, carbuncles of fiery scarlet with tremulous four-rayed stars, flame-red cinnamon-stones, orange and violent spinels, and amethysts with their alternate layers of ruby and sapphire. . . . Then he turned his attention to embroideries. . . . As he investigated the subject—and he always had an extraordinary faculty of becoming absolutely absorbed for the moment in whatever he took up—he was almost saddened by the reflection of the ruin that Time brought on beautiful and wonderful things. He, at any rate, had escaped that. . . . How different it was with material things! Where had they

passed to? Where was the great crocus-coloured robe, on which the gods fought against the giants, that had been worked by brow girls for the pleasure of Athena? Where the huge velarium that Nero had stretched across the Colosseum at Rome, that Titan sail of purple on which was represented the starry sky, and Apollo driving a chariot drawn by white gilt-reined steeds? . . . He loved to stroll through the gaunt cold picture-gallery of his country house and look at the various portraits of those whose blood flowed in his veins. Here was Philip Herbert described by Francis Osborne . . . as one who was "caressed by the Court for his handsome face, which kept him not long company." . . . Here, in gold-embroidered red doublet, jewelled surcoat, and gilt-edged ruff and wrist-bands, stood Sir Anthony Sherard, with his silver-and-black armour piled at his feet. . . . Here, from the fading canvas, smiled Lady Elizabeth Devereux, in her gauze hood, pearl stomacher, and pink slashed sleeves. . . . George Willoughby, with his powdered hair and fantastic patches . . . his mother with her Lady Hamilton face, and her moist wine-dashed lips.[61]

"Ah Dorian. . . . What an exquisite life you have led! You have drunk deeply of everything"—and yet so little of anything.[62] So glittering is the itinerary of his world tour that we may neglect to notice how short is each stay; so infinite the plenitude of his exquisite life that we may fail to observe how limited the contact of his eye with any of its specific elements. The pathos of their passing that occasionally occurs to Dorian Gray as he glimpses first one and then another of this gorgeous multitude—"Here was . . . one whose handsome face . . . kept him not long company"; a sense of pathos that doubles with the schadenfreude of one full of confidence that his own luster will never fail—"How different it was material things! Where had they passed to?"—offers an objective correlative for the brevity of his own intercourse with each of them. "[H]e always had an extraordinary facility of becoming absolutely absorbed *for the moment* in whatever he took up"—a moment that the list where it is mentioned conspires to make seem shorter still, not only because of the contrast between the brief finitude of a moment and the virtual infinity suggested by a roster whose end is nowhere in sight, but also because, as with any item on a list, and especially one this long, it is hard to resist the tendency to reduce the

[61] Ibid., p. 103.
[62] Ibid., pp. 147–54.

thing itself to nothing more than that, and thus to imagine that each lasts no longer than the length of time it takes to read or to say it. And its hard to resist the tendency to compress a list this long for the simpler reason as well that we have so much to get through.

The fantastic multitude through which Dorian Gray wanders, as vast in scope as the stops he makes along the way are slight in duration, gathers together all aspects of "the sensuous life." Even the warning issued near the outset of this tour, against "the error of arresting [one's] *intellectual* development by any formal acceptance of creed or system," is engulfed in that world, and not only because of the suggestive materiality of the figure to which it attached—"mistaking, for a house in which to live, an inn that is but suitable for the sojourn of a night, or for a few hours of a night in which there are no stars and the moon is in travail"—but also because the warning is prompted in the first place less by the attractions of any "creed or system" attached to "the Roman Catholic communion" than by the feel of kneeling on "cold marble pavement," the sight of the "priest, in his stiff flowered dalmatic" and the "fuming censers, that the grave boys, in their lace and scarlet, tossed into the air like great gilt flowers."[63] The brave new world that Dorian Gray discovers in the wake of Sybil Vane speaks to various senses, but it engages in particular the one that has concerned us here. Above all, the wonder of this world makes you see; the scent of perfume and the sound of music give way to a spectacle that seduces the eyes: "grave yellow-shawled Tunisians"; "slim turbaned Indians" "crouching upon scarlet mats"; "rose-pink and wine-yellow topazes," "carbuncles of fiery scarlet."

As with the epic forest or urban center, an atmosphere of menace, thin at first, but thickening the longer one looks at it into grotesque spectacles, clings to this spectacular arcade. Thus in the account of Dorian Gray's musical phase, the vague threat lurking in the sight of "grinning negroes beating . . . upon copper drums," and "slim turbaned Indians" "crouching upon scarlet mats" turns before our fixed eyes into "flutes of human bones . . . and a huge cylindrical drum, covered with the skins of great serpents. . . . monsters, things of bestial shape." The spectacle of jewels, when one looks long enough, reveals "a serpent . . . with eyes of

---

[63] Ibid., pp. 209–10.

real jacinth"; "snakes 'with collars of real emeralds growing on the their backs' "; "a gem in the brain" of "a dragon"; "a white stone taken from the brain of a newly-killed toad"; the "bezoar," "found in the heart of the Arabian deer"; and "rose-coloured pearls in the mouths of the dead." As if our trained sight is itself somehow responsible, the shapes become fearful as our vision lingers here, like the shot in the horror movie where the normal image metamorphosizes before our captive eyes into the harrowing one: a familiar face becomes a hateful alien; a recovered vehicle a sick smile, and then a mother's skull. As if our trained sight is somehow responsible? Such a sense of complicity comes from the guilty knowledge that if our eyes are captive to these scenes, they are captive to our own desire to keep looking at them, the pleasure driven by the dread of what they will see: the fatal car accident, say, and its sickening contortions, or the picture of Dorian Gray, from which, despite his resolutions—"He himself would not see it. Why should he watch the hideous corruption of his soul?"—he can't finally tear himself away.

As if to warn against the tendency to keep looking, there lurk subliminal messages in the midst of the great exhibition situated at the center of *Dorian Gray*. These messages work to associate the tenacious eye with pain, illness, and death—"the mysterious *juruparis* of the Rio Negro Indians that youths may not see till they have been subjected to fasting and scourging"; the sorry sight of "Domitian . . . wandering through a corridor lined with marble mirrors, looking round with haggard eyes for a reflection of the dagger that was to end his days" and of "Charles VI, who . . . when his brain had sickened and grown strange, could only be soothed by Saracen cards painted with the images of Love and Death and Madness"—sights like the picture of Dorian Gray, in which the painter is presented with the results of his "curious artistic idolatry."

But how, despite any such discouragement, is one to avoid the seduction of the eyes, the lure, for example, of "all those strange terrible figures that had passed across the stage of the world and made sin so marvelous": "Tiberius in a garden of Capri, reading the shameful books of Elephantis, while dwarfs and peacocks strutted round him"; or "Caligula . . . carousing with the green-shirted jockeys in their stables"; and supped in an ivory manger with a jewel-fronted horse"; or "the young Cardinal

Archbishop of Florence," "whose beauty was equaled only by his debauchery, and who . . . gilded a boy that he might serve at the feast as Ganymede"; or "in his trimmed jerkin and jewelled cap and acanthus-like curls, Grifonetto Baglioni, who slew Astorre with his bride, and Simonetto with his page, and whose comeliness was such that, as he lay dying in the yellow piazza of Perugia, those who hated him could not choose but weep"?

Rather like the moral lessons that Wilde sought to attach to his novel after the fact of its scandalous effects, any caution to avert the gaze dwells uneasily with the appeal of what it warns against. How to avoid the arrest of the eyes by the undeniable lure of the comely form? The arrest of eyes weak enough to weep at the loss of the beautiful face, no matter how vicious? Eyes, which, like the author whose appetite for self-destruction has proven the heaviest of the imputations lodged against him, are weak enough to want arrest?

> CECILY: Miss Prism says that all good looks are a snare.
> ALGERNON: They are a snare that every sensible man would like to be
> caught in.[64]

We have seen eyes like these before: they are the ones susceptible to the engrossments of the charismatic spectacle, so caught and kept that the gravest measures are necessary to free them. To break the line of vision that binds him to the sight of her, the young Syrian must fall on his sword. Nothing less could release him from a bondage as enthralling as any biblical captivity. Even Herod, his own vision somewhat less attached than the languorous eyes of his soldier, must resort to the most extreme measures in order to terminate the arresting spectacle of Salome:

> HEROD: [*Turning round and seeing Salome*] Kill that woman!
> [*The soldiers rush forward and crush beneath their shields Salome*][65]

By the time they arrive, though, the damage is done: the shields that remove Salome from the scene can do nothing to prevent the catastrophe that the sight of her has already caused: not like the one with which

---

[64] Oscar Wilde, *The Importance of Being Earnest*, in *Major Works*, p. 505.
[65] *Salome*, p. 329.

Perseus deflects the paralyzing gaze of Medusa, nor, for that matter, to shift our sights from far to near, like the ordinary pressure—hard to tell from the mere pleasure—we all know to circulate in a crowd; a pressure to circulate as casual as the tendency that keeps us on one side of a busy sidewalk, but also as consequential as the one that keeps us on one side of a busy highway; the casual pressure to circulate that spirits us away from even the most arresting sight before its too late. This pressure to circulate is as light as the sense of hurry incited by the sight of a crowd or a scan of a list, as subtle as those discouragements that, like the habit of discretion that they help to form, take the tack of what goes without saying—the slight apprehension that prompts us to look away in time, the mild pain of embarrassment when we fail to do so. The armor of Athena is no more effective against the depredations of the compelling vision than the habit of social circulation by which our contact with any particular person, no matter how arresting, is necessarily limited, the habit of circulation that protects Dorian Gray against the "insolent pose" and "moist lips" that we will encounter with him now in his gallery of portraits. If the tendency to circulate makes the dullness of individual members of society bearable—the dullness which Lady Bracknell admits, "It is my last reception, and one wants something that will encourage conversation, particularly at the end of the season when everyone has practically said whatever they had to say, which, in most cases, was probably not much"—it also insulates us from the fascination of individual members, as well, the fascinations exerted by the likes of "the second Lord Beckenham. . . . [h]ow proud and handsome he was, with his chestnut curls and insolent pose! What passions had he bequeathed? . . . The star of the Garter glittered upon his breast,"

> and his mother with . . . her moist wine-dashed lips—he knew what he got from her. He had got from her his beauty, and his passion for the beauty of others. She laughed at him in her loose Bacchante dress. There were vine leaves in her hair. The purple spilled from the cup she was holding. The carnations of the painting had withered, but the eyes were still wonderful in their depth and brilliancy of colour. They seemed to follow him wherever he went.[66]

[66] *Dorian Gray,* p. 155.

His mother's eyes may seem to come alive, like those in the picture of Dorian Gray himself, and follow him, but all they can catch is the sight of his back. His own eyes have moved on to the next picture, and thus, in the blink of an eye, the spell of seduction is broken; the erotic aristocracy whose heraldry is the insolent pose and the mocking laugh disappear; its apparatus of entrapment is shrunk to eyes fixed themselves now on the receding figure of the one who got away.

The vision of Dorian Gray is developed now, trained like the urban eyes made ready for the subtle, or at least silent, combat of the sexual olympic played out on city streets, where victory is achieved by averting one's own before one's opponent has a chance to avert his; the glance that knows how to look just long enough to catch the glance of the other and then leave it hanging, rather than be left hanging itself; the eyes whose habit of deflecting a striking sight—"[h]ow proud and handsome he was, with his chestnut curls and insolent pose"—gains courage from the prospect of countless others coming down the street. This presumption of plenty more reflected in the haughty eye is the luxury of the urban gaze adapted to city crowds, and, as well, the urbane one that has become acultured to the congestion of spectacle available "[o]n a shelf of the bookcase behind you:"

> on a shelf of the bookcase behind you stands the *Divine Comedy*. . . . We . . .walk with grave Virgil through 'the valley of the shadow of death,' and lo! . . .with pity or with joy behold the horror of another world. The hypocrites go by, with their painted faces and their cowls of gilded lead. . . . we watch the heretic rending his flesh, and the glutton lashed by the rain. . . . Through the dim purple air fly those who have stained the world with the beauty of their sin, and in the pit of loathsome disease, dropsy-stricken and swollen of body into the semblance of a monstrous lute, lies Adamo di Brescia, the coiner of false coin. . . . We are fascinated by their shame, and loiter, till Virgil chides us and leads us away.[67]

Virgil need chide us only once. The lesson not to linger is the one easiest to learn amongst the precepts of Wilde's Dante—a lesson that, along with the rest of what is promulgated by *The Divine Comedy*, is taught in the

---

[67] Oscar Wilde, "The Critic as Artist," in *Major Works*, p. 270–71.

153

practice of reading the poem. Unlike other such practices, though, like those that require empathic ordeals as difficult as any task set out for the ancient hero—the labor of pity or the labor of its refusal, the vicissitudes of fear and the agonies of repentance that we, along with Dante are obliged to undertake in order to rise. Alongside the pains that we must take to learn the grammar of ascent, there is no lesson harder than learning to shift the eye to a new scene or a new line.

But this lesson is easily forgotten when the visual affluence through which it is conducted disappears. The renovation of the eye can last only as long as the lustrous crowd, the one assumed by the haughty eyes of the urban promenade, glamorous with the expectation that they dwell in a setting congested with good looks. Such eyes are no match for a city of a single spectacle; they can hardly maintain their composure when there is only one person on the street or in the room who draws the gaze. The story is simply this:

> Two months ago I went to a crush. . . . You know how we artists have to show ourselves in society from time to time, just to remind the public we are not savages. With an evening coat and a white-tie, as you told me once, anybody, even a stock-broker can gain a reputation for being civilized. Well, after I had been in the room about ten minutes talking to huge overdressed dowagers and tedious academicians, I suddenly became conscious that someone was looking at me. I turned half-way round, and saw Dorian Gray for the first time. When our eyes met, I felt that I was growing pale. A curious sensation of terror came over me. I knew that I had come face to face with someone whose mere personality was so fascinating that, if I allowed it to do so, it would absorb my whole soul, my very art itself.[68]

"I suddenly became conscious that someone was looking at me," Basil Hallward reports, but he could also admit that he suddenly became conscious that he was looking at someone. He talks to huge overdressed dowagers and tedious Academicians, but sees only Dorian Gray. His are the only eyes that Basil Hallward's eyes meet, his the only face that his faces. As sure as the effects on consumer behavior exerted by the classic monop-

---

[68] *Dorian Gray*, p. 53.

oly, the casual glance dissolves into the arrested gaze the moment that all available visual splendor is gathered into the luster of a single figure.

•   •   •   •   •

But if the turn to the crowd that we have witnessed so far proves insufficient to stand against the arrest of the eye by the power of the charismatic spectacle, a more abstract attention to the crowd provides a final solution. This study of the crowd extends beyond the defensive strategy we have already analyzed that functions by broadening the field of vision, and thus freeing the gaze, but only until the next charismatic character appears on the scene. Rather the turn to the crowd in Wilde that we will take up now works to narrow the field of vision, ultimately to the vanishing point, and thus to free the gaze from the risks of exposure once and for all.

We can begin to take the measure of this endgame of the visual field by comparing the eyes involved in it with the urban ones we have glanced at before. Hardened by the stimulations of the city, those eyes will often appear to see no one at all, as if the habit of minimal contact with any single individual engenders an astigmatism that, in its final stages, comes to block the sight of individuals altogether. Replace the haughty stare with the happy eye, a negative image, from which individuals have been excluded, with a positive one, where they have been absorbed: this is the more sophisticated sight of the crowd in Wilde's book. For while his student continues to recognize, if only in passing, individual images drift by on a "river of changing faces" in the visionary arcade through which he wanders,[69] the teacher has graduated to a vision of the crowd in which all such residue has been dissolved; a vision of the crowd at the center of modernity; a vision of the crowd like the one that Siegfried Kracauer calls the mass ornament:

> These products of American distraction factories are no longer individual girls, but indissoluble girl clusters whose movements are demonstrations of mathematics. . . . One need only glance at the screen to learn that the ornaments are composed of thousands of bodies. . . . These extravagant spectacles, which are staged by many sorts of people and not just girls and stadium

---

[69] Joni Mitchell, "Trouble Child" from *Court and Spark* [1973] (Crazy Crow Music).

crowds, have long since become an established form. . . . They are composed
of elements that are mere building blocks and nothing more. The construction of the edifice depends on the size of the stones and their number. It is
the mass that is employed here.[70]

As with the kaleidoscopic formations that Kracauer describes here, or the
formation of clouds that Lord Henry sees while himself at work forming
individuals into categories—"tilting his hat back, and looking up at the
little clouds that, like ravelled skeins of glossy white silk, were drifting
across the hollowed turquoise of the summer sky . . .' I choose my friends
for their good looks, my acquaintances for their good characters, and my
enemies for their good intellects'—all that is individual dissolves by the
light of his eyes into the distant haze of the generic.

  Such a spectacle is the fruit of the theory whose practice Lord
Henry renders as so many species of promiscuity, the theory he calls "the
science" of "human life"—the human science whose first methodological
principle is the subordination of the particular person to the task of knowing the social whole; the conscription of the individual as case-study; the
relegation of the one to the Many rather than, as in the sight of Salome,
the many to the One. This attenuated view of the crowd culminates in a
vision where more than the details of individual faces are lost, a view of the
crowd that, despite its vivid colors, can hardly be counted as a vision at all:

> As [Dorian Gray] left the room, Lord Henry's heavy eyelids drooped, and he
> began to think. Certainly few people had ever interested him so much as
> Dorian Gray, and yet the lad's mad adoration of someone else caused him not
> the slightest pang of annoyance or jealousy. He was pleased by it. It made him
> an interesting study. He had always been enthralled by the methods of natural
> science, but the ordinary subject-matter of that science had seemed to him
> trivial and of no import. And so he had begun by vivisecting himself, as he
> had ended by vivisecting others. Human life—that appeared to him the one
> thing worth investigating. Compared to it there was nothing of any value. It
> was true that as one watched life in its curious crucible of pain and pleasure,

[70] Siegfried Kracauer, "The Mass Ornament," in *The Mass Ornament: Weimar Essays*,
translated, edited, and with an Introduction by Thomas Y. Levin (Cambridge: Harvard University Press, 1995), p. 76.

one could not wear over one's face a mask of glass, nor keep the sulphurous fumes from troubling the brain and making the imagination turbid with monstrous fancies and misshapen dreams. There were poisons so subtle that one had to sicken of them. There were maladies so strange that one had to pass through them if one sought to understand their nature. And, yet, what a great reward one received! How wonderful the whole world became to one! To note the curious hard logic of passion, and the emotional coloured life of the intellect—to observe where they met, and where they separated, at what point they were in unison, and at what point they were at discord—there was a delight in that! What matter what the cost was? One could never pay too high a price for any sensation.

He was conscious—and the thought brought a gleam of pleasure into his brown agate eyes—that it was through certain words of his . . . that Dorian Gray's soul had turned to this white girl and bowed in worship before her.[71]

This sensational human science provides the comprehensive cover for the eye that the work of art, by means of which Basil Hallward seeks to deflect his gaze from the sight of others, cannot: the work of art in which the artist, despite his craftiest machinations, is still liable to be caught looking. For here, there is no gaze to surprise; here vision has been suspended altogether, rather than cast in a remote anterior; here, finally, the subject who apprehends need never fear that he will be caught looking himself. The science of human life, "the curious hard logic of passion, and the emotional coloured life of the intellect," is a metaphysical spectacle whose elements are perceived by methods beyond the faculty of vision. In a paradox worthy of Wilde, but also strange for one as enamored as he of the visible, this spectacle gains color and texture as it fades from view, as a view, as the "life" that one "watches" gives way to the "hard logic of passion" and "the emotional coloured life of the intellect," whose interactions one notes and observes as if from within, but not actually so, the laboratory of chemist or anatomist.

To be sure, such abstraction from the sense of sight is hardly abstract in any other sense: like the private detective or the counterinsurgent who, in the line of duty, needs not only to take on, but also take in, the

---

[71] *Dorian Gray,* pp. 90–91.

criminal or anticolonial elements he seeks to investigate, the scientist who "watche[s] life" cannot "wear over" his "face a mask of glass." "There were poisons so subtle that to know their properties one had to sicken of them. . . . maladies so strange that one had to pass through them if one sought to understand their nature." Nevertheless, as comprehensive as the assignments of the course set out here may seem, it requires nothing from the sense of sight. Where visual material is absorbed by the student of general human life, it is done by a means of osmosis quite apart from the avenue of the eye, the process by which "the sulphurous fumes" arising from the "life" that one "watches" come to "troubl[e] the brain and mak[e] the imagination turbid with monstrous fancies and misshapen dreams." According to the science that Lord Henry sets forth here, the spectacle of human life is never to be perceived by the naked eye, but rather admitted by other means: "One should absorb the colour of life, but one should never remember its details."[72]

And what Wilde's psychologist enshrines as doctrine, his student practices without thinking when he considers the spectacular crowd through which he makes his way in chapter 11:

> There was a horrible fascination in them all. He saw them at night, and they troubled his imagination in the day. The Renaissance knew of strange manners of poisoning—poisoning by a helmet and a lighted torch, by an embroidered glove and a jewelled fan, by a gilded pomander and by an amber chain. Dorian Gray had been poisoned by a book. There were moments when he looked on evil simply as a mode through which he could realize his conception of the beautiful.[73]

These are the last words of the chapter, and they refer to its final section, the fantastic images of decadence we have already witnessed, fantastic images projected by the yellow book from whose "influence" he "could not free himself." Thus the spectacle of the crowd whose afterimage he "sees" is available only by means of the imagination's eye, whose abstract medium (a plain book: not even, as it is elsewhere, wrapped in a yellow cover) is lit up by its contrast with the brief but flashy exhibition of poisonings where

[72] Ibid., p. 123.
[73] Ibid., p. 156–57.

it is incongruously located. What Dorian Gray sees at night and what troubles his imagination by day enters through the abstract avenue of reading, which may resemble the sensory outlets—the nose, the mouth, of course the ear—where poison typically finds a way in, but it avoids traversing the field of vision. Even in those "moments" when the path by which the vision of the crowd that enters the mind's eye appears to verge on vision itself, "moments when he looked on evil," the object viewed, as if by virtue of some fail-safe protective mechanism, ceases altogether during the course of the looking to be a matter that can be seen; as if by an automatic response to the pressure of the gaze, the object ceases to be an ambiguous combination of the sensory and the abstract and metamorphoses into a matter of thought alone, the instrument of a metaphysical construction: "There were moments when he looked on evil simply as a mode through which he could realize his conception of the beautiful."

"One could never pay too high a price for any sensation." Even if the price for such sensations is the dearest of senses. For the eyes adjusted to the crowd are hardened after all. Their light is now the flicker of pure speculation: "He was conscious—and the thought brought a gleam of pleasure into his brown agate eyes." If these eyes bring on a flickering vision of those other eyes that a sea-change turned to pearls, this is in part because softer ones seem so unnecessary now, as if the labor of thought that composes the abstract spectacle of the social scientist brings with it first the dejection (the "droop[ing]") and then the disabling of the natural eyes, as if the now useless ocular organ is slated to suffer the extinction assigned by the drama of evolution to all that is obsolete.[74]

These agate eyes are more stunning still when we reflect upon the character to whom they are attached. For these are the eyes of Wilde's most devoted spokesman for the wonders of the visible world, wonders such as the human face divine, ranged as first amongst equals with "the great facts of the world, like sunlight, or spring-time, or the reflection in

---

[74] The story to be discerned in the drift away from the field of the visual in this passage is a brief but telling instance of the "ocularphobic discourse" that Martin Jay has located at the center of modern French thought. See Martin Jay, *Downcast Eyes: The Denigration of Vision in Twentieth-Century French Thought* (Berkeley: University of California, 1993), p. 15.

dark waters of that silver shell we call the moon."[75] These are the eyes of one most at home admiring all that they see rather than, say, those of the hard scientist who walks on and off the stage of *The Picture of Dorian Gray* only once, "an extremely clever young man, though he had no real appreciation of the visual arts." Only a sacrifice distinctly more drastic than those Lord Henry habitually eschews, no matter how alluring the temptation—"to get back my youth, I would do anything except take exercise, get up early, or be respectable"—proves sufficient to defend against the embarrassments endured by the arrested gaze. His defense against a danger which a more blatantly anxious contemporary calls "the possibilities of faces" that, is always "one of the notes of the scene,"[76] compels him to abandon what is elsewhere all he wants: "All I want . . . is to look at life." Less public, this sacrifice of the eyes is no less apocalyptic than the one exacted from all the world in the general eclipse that Herod orders at the end of *Salome* so that his own will cease to be exposed: "I will not look at things. I will not suffer things to look at me. Put out the torches! Hide the moon! Hide the stars!" "I have sorrows . . . of my own, that even you know nothing of,"[77] Lord Henry confesses the last time we see him in *The Picture of Dorian Gray*. Surely amongst them is the wincing of the eyes at the threat of their mortification, whose ultimate scope is nowhere in sight.

[75] *Dorian Gray*, p. 64.
[76] Henry James, *The Golden Bowl* [1904] (New York: Penquin, 1985), p. 43.
[77] *Dorian Gray*, p. 209.

INDEX

action, 99–104, 106, 111
adultery, 82
advertising, 83–84, 106, 126
Aestheticism, 44, 48, 83
aesthetics, 34–35, 50–52, 83–84, 106, 117–19, 132
Anderson, Amanda, 33n.71
Anderson, Benedict, 124
Arendt, Hannah, 100n.26, 103
"arrested eyes." *See* gazes
artists and aesthetes, 36–37, 39, 47
"art of the self." *See* self-realization
asceticism, 11
Auden, W. H., 71n

Barthes, Roland, 14, 51–52
Baudelaire, Charles-Pierre, 77, 116, 130
Baudrillard, Jean, 114n, 116
beauty. *See* youth and beauty
Benjamin, Walter, 107–8, 130
"Birthday of the Infanta, The," 97
black men, sexuality of, 46
Bloom, Allen, 86
body, 25, 134; beauty and youth of the, 54–57, 65–69, 83, 88–89; fatigue, boredom, and the, 71–77, 86; stigma and the, 63–64
boredom, 35, 71–89, 126
Bourdieu, Pierre, 61n, 99
Bowlby, Rachel, 83
"Bunburying," 4, 43, 50
Butler, Judith, 61–62, 93

Carlyle, Thomas, 108, 111–12
Castiglione, Baldassare, 60n.12
charismatic figures. *See* gazes
Chesterton, G. K., 48
coercion, 41, 46–47. *See also* power
coming out stories, 41–42

Communism, 95
consumption and consumer demand, 30–32, 80–84, 89, 126–27
control. *See* self-management, sexual
cosmopolitanism, 33–34
Craft, Christopher, 22
"Critic as Artist, The," 34–35, 47, 99–106, 108–10, 112–13, 117, 119–20, 153
crowds, 2, 143–150, 152, 154–156, 158–159

death, 76–79, 84
"Decay of Lying, The," 18n.28, 48, 79
de-essentialism, 90–93, 101n, 114–20
"De Profundis," 128
desire-lite, 44–45, 48–50. *See also* de-essentialism
detachment. *See* indifference
disinterestedness, 34–35, 117–18. *See also* indifference
Divine Comedy, The (Dante), 153
double-lives, 42–43
Dr. Jekyl and Mr. Hyde (Stevenson), 42
Dracula (Stoker), 13

economics, 28, 30–34, 126–27
Edelman, Lee, 91
essentialism. *See* de-essentialism
exoticism, 46–48
"eye for the crowd." *See* gazes

faces, 64
Fanon, Frantz, 46
fatigue, 72–73, 75–77, 86
fear, 42
female sexuality, 11–14
flirtation, 18

161

theatrical agency, 57, 61–64, 69–70
Tyler, Carole Ann, 44
"tyranny of want." *See* starvation

uncertainty, 22
urbanity. *See* cosmopolitanism

Veblen, Thorstein, 96, 97
voluntarism, 43, 54

Weber, Max, 28n, 30, 76n.12, 108, 114
Woman of No Importance, A, 98
work ethic, 3, 30, 93–114, 118. *See also* action; idleness

"Young King, The," 142
youth and beauty, 54, 64–69, 83, 85–89, 123, 132